THE SECRET
OF THE ROSARY

"One Day through the Rosary and Scapular
I will save the world."
—Blessed Virgin Mary to Saint Dominic

★ ★ ★

THE SECRET
OF THE ROSARY

by
Saint Louis Mary De Montfort

Translator
Mary Barbour, T.O.P

ISBN: 978-1-63923-231-4

Printed: June 2022

Cover Art By: Amit Paul

Published and Distributed By: Lushena Books
607 Country Club Drive, Unit E
Bensenville, IL 60106
www.lushenabooksinc.com/books

ISBN: 978-1-63923-231-4

THE SECRET
OF THE ROSARY

by
Saint Louis Mary De Montfort

Translator
Mary Barbour, T.O.P

Contents

Part I
WHAT THE ROSARY IS

Part II
HOW TO RECITE IT

Preface

BIOGRAPHERS have already told us much about St. Louis De Montfort and the Rosary; now, with this first English edition of THE SECRET OF THE ROSARY, we can listen to Montfort speaking for himself. Drawing upon his own experience as well as upon the experience of others,[1] he endeavors to bring home to the reader, "in a simple and straightforward manner," as he himself tells us, the authentic message of the Rosary; namely, that it is a veritable school of Christian life. He sees it as including essentially the meditation of the mysteries of the life, death and glory of Jesus and Mary, with a view not only to honoring but especially imitating their virtues as held up to our consideration in each mystery.

For our Saint, the Rosary was not simply a method of prayer: it was his most effective tool and weapon in his apostolic work. Fittingly has the Church called him an "Extraordinary preacher of the Rosary." He preached it in season and out of season; established it in every parish where he gave a mission[2] and judged the fruits of the mission by the subsequent perseverance in its recitation. There was no limit to the power of the Rosary and to it he attributed much of his success with sinners. "Let me but place my rosary around a sinner's neck," he was wont to say, "and he will not escape me."

A Dominican Tertiary himself, De Montfort represents the best in the Dominican Rosary tradition. Speaking of our Saint's contribution to the Rosary, Father R. Poupon, well known Dominican writer says, "Montfort's genius prolongs

---

1. See "Tenth Rose" for some of his sources.
2. It is estimated that he enrolled over 100,000 persons in the Rosary Confraternity. (Le Crom, S.M.M. "St. L-M. de Montfort" Ch. XV, p. 311.)

in one straight line that of Blessed Alan de la Roche and of St. Dominic. He completes them by bringing forth a personal grace and interpretation." Commenting on De Montfort's book, Father Willam says, "It goes far beyond mere research. We might say that it contains everything that can be said about the rosary, about its content and form, its real worth, about the instruction necessary for its appreciation and use."[3]

THE SECRET OF THE ROSARY was written almost two and a half centuries ago, it is true, but it has lost none of its freshness and timeliness. Indeed, today, in the light of the specific requests of Our Lady of Fatima, it will be doubly welcomed by all true clients of, Our Lady. We feel confident that it will bring many souls to a better understanding of the Rosary not only as a prayer but especially as a way of spiritual life.   THE EDITORS

---

3. F. M. Willam, The Rosary: Its History and Meaning, Benziger Bros., 1952, p. 115.

THE FRONT COVER of the SORROWFUL AND IMMAC-
ULATE HEART OF MARY. This picture, somewhat mysterious in its origin, was discovered at the time of the 1918
armistice in the cellar of the boarding school where Berthe
Petit, a humble Franciscan Tertiary, had been educated. After
the troops had departed, one of the Bernardine nuns in putting
things in order found a piece of cardboard on which was
pasted a pornographic picture and she tore it off to consign it
to flames. To her astonishment she found that it covered this
beautiful representation of the Blessed Virgin! It seems to
combine the art of both the Eastern and the Western Rites. The
facial features resemble those of the well known Pieta. Prayer
before this picture has brought signal favors.

Confided by Our Lord to Berthe Petit: "Teach souls to love
the Heart of My Mother pierced by the very sorrow which
pierced Mine." (Dec. 25, 1909).

"The Heart of My Mother has the right to be called Sorrowful and I wish this title placed before that of Immaculate
because she has won it herself. The Church has defined in the
case of My Mother what I Myself had ordained—her Immaculate Conception. This right which My Mother has to a title of
justice is now, according to My express wish, to be known and
universally accepted. She has earned it by her identification
with My sorrows; by her sufferings; by her sacrifices and her
immolation in Calvary endured in perfect correspondence with
My grace for the salvation of mankind . . ." (Sept. 8, 1911).

"It is hearts that must be changed. This will be accom-
plished only by the Devotion proclaimed, explained, preached
and recommended everywhere. Recourse to My Mother under
this title I wish for her universally, is the last help I shall give
before the end of time." (July 2, 1940).

A White Rose

DEAR MINISTERS of the Most High, you my fellow priests who preach the truth of God and who teach the gospel to all nations, let me give you this little book as a white rose that I would like you to keep. The truths contained in it are set forth in a very simple and straightforward manner as you will see. Please keep them in your heart so that you yourselves may make a practice of the Holy Rosary and taste its fruit; and please have them always on your lips too so that you will always preach the Rosary and thus convert others by teaching them the excellence of this holy devotion.

I beg of you to beware of thinking of the Rosary as something of little importance—as do ignorant people and even several great but proud scholars. Far from being insignificant, the Rosary is a priceless treasure which is inspired by God.

Almighty God has given it to you because He wants you to use it as a means to convert the most hardened sinners and the most obstinate heretics. He has attached to it grace in this life and glory in the next. The Saints have said it faithfully and the Popes have endorsed it.

When the Holy Spirit has revealed this secret to a priest and director of souls, how blessed is that priest! For the vast majority of people fail to know this secret or else only know it superficially. If such a priest really understands this secret he will say the Rosary every day and will encourage others to say it. God and His Blessed Mother will pour abundant grace into his soul, so that he may become God's instrument for His glory; and his word, though simple, will do more good in one month than that of other preachers in several years.

Therefore, my dear brethren and fellow priests, it will not be enough for us to preach this devotion to others; we must practice it ourselves. Even if we firmly believed in the importance of the Holy Rosary but never said it ourselves, people could hardly be expected to act upon our advice, for no one can give what he does not have: "Jesus began to do and to teach." (*Acts* 1:1). We ought to pattern ourselves on Our Blessed Lord, Who began by practicing what He preached. We ought to emulate Saint Paul who knew and preached nothing but Jesus Crucified. This is really and truly what you will be doing if you preach the Holy Rosary. It is not just a conglomeration of Our Fathers and Hail Marys, but on the contrary it is a divine summary of the mysteries of the life, Passion, death and glory of Jesus and Mary.

I could tell you at great length of the grace God gave me to know by experience the effectiveness of the preaching of the Holy Rosary and of how I have seen, with my own eyes, the most wonderful conversions it has brought about. I would gladly tell you all these things if I thought that it would move you to preach this beautiful devotion, in spite of the fact that priests are not in the habit of doing so these days. But instead of all this I think it will be quite enough for this little summary that I am writing if I tell you a few ancient but authentic stories about the Holy Rosary. These excerpts really go to prove what I have outlined for the faithful in French.

A Red Rose

For Sinners

POOR MEN AND WOMEN who are sinners, I, a greater sinner than you, wish to give to you this rose—a crimson one, because the Precious Blood of Our Lord has fallen upon it. Please God that it will bring true fragrance into your lives—but above all may it save you from the danger that you are in. Every day unbelievers and unrepentant sinners cry: "Let us crown ourselves with roses." (*Wis.* 2:8) But our cry should be: "Let us crown ourselves with roses of the Most Holy Rosary."

How different are theirs from ours! Their roses are pleasures of the flesh, worldly honors and passing riches which wilt and decay in no time, but ours, which are the Our Father and Hail Mary which we have said devoutly over and over again and to which we have added good penitential acts, will never wilt or die and they will be just as exquisite thousands of years from now as they are today.

On the contrary, sinners' roses only look like roses, while in point of fact they are cruel thorns which prick them during life by giving them pangs of conscience, at their death they pierce them with bitter regret and, still worse, in eternity, they turn to burning shafts of anger and despair. But if our roses have thorns, they are the thorns of Jesus Christ Who changes them into roses. If our roses prick us, it is only for a short time—and only in order to cure the illness of sin and to save our souls.

So by all means we should eagerly crown ourselves with these roses from Heaven, and recite the entire Rosary every day, that is to say three Rosaries each of five decades which are like three little wreaths or crowns of flowers: and there are two reasons for doing this: First of all to honor the three crowns of Jesus and Mary—Jesus' crown of grace at the time of His incarnation, His crown of thorns during His Passion and His crown of glory in Heaven, and of course the three-fold crown which the Most Blessed Trinity gave Mary in Heaven.

Secondly, we should do this so that we ourselves may receive three crowns from Jesus and Mary. The first is a crown of merit during our lifetime, the second, a crown of peace at our death, and the third, a crown of glory in Heaven.

If you say the Rosary faithfully until death, I do assure you that, in spite of the gravity of your sins "you shall receive a never fading crown of glory." (*1 Ptr.* 5:4). Even if you are on the brink of damnation, even if you have one foot in Hell, even if you have sold your soul to the devil as sorcerers do who practice black magic, and even if you are a heretic as obstinate as a devil, sooner or later you will be converted and will amend your life and save your soul, if—and mark well what I say—if you say the Holy Rosary devoutly every day until death for the purpose of knowing the truth and obtaining contrition and pardon for your sins.

In this book there are several stories of great sinners who were converted through the power of the Holy Rosary. Please read and meditate upon them.

A Mystical Rose Tree

For Devout Souls

GOOD AND DEVOUT SOULS, who walk in the light of the Holy Spirit: I do not think that you will mind my giving you this little mystical rose tree which comes straight from Heaven and which is to be planted in the garden of your soul. It cannot possibly harm the sweet smelling flowers of your contemplations; for it is a heavenly tree and its scent is beautiful. It will not in the least interfere with your carefully planned flower beds; for, being itself all pure and well-ordered, it inclines all to order and purity. If it is carefully watered and properly attended to every day it will grow to such a marvelous height and its branches will have such a wide span that, far from hindering your other devotions, it will maintain and perfect them.

Of course you understand what I mean, since you are spiritually-minded; this mystical rose tree is Jesus and Mary in life, death and eternity; its green leaves are the Joyous Mysteries, the thorns the Sorrowful ones and the flowers, the Glorious Mysteries of Jesus and Mary. The buds are the childhood of Jesus and Mary, and the open blooms show us both of them in their sufferings, and the full-blown roses symbolize Jesus and Mary in their triumph and glory.

A rose delights us because of its beauty—so here we have Jesus and Mary in the Joyous Mysteries. Its thorns are sharp, and prick, which makes us think of them in the Sorrowful Mysteries, and last of all its perfume is so sweet that everyone loves it, and this fragrance symbolizes their Glorious Mysteries.

So please do not scorn this beautiful and heavenly tree, but plant it with your own hands in the garden of your soul, making the resolution to say your Rosary every day. By saying it daily and by doing good works you will be tending your tree, watering it, hoeing the earth around it. Eventually you will see that this little seed which I have given you, and which seems so very small now, will grow into a tree so great that the birds of heaven, i.e., predestinate and contemplative souls, will dwell in it and make their nests there. Its shade will shelter them from the scorching heat of the sun and its great height will keep them safe from the wild beasts on the ground. And best of all, they will feed upon the tree's fruit—which is none other than our adorable Jesus, to whom be honor and glory forever and ever. Amen. So be it.

GOD ALONE

A Rosebud

For Little Children

D EAR LITTLE FRIENDS, this beautiful rosebud is for you; it is one of the beads of your Rosary, and it may seem to you to be such a tiny thing. But if you only knew how precious this bead is! This wonderful bud will open out into a gorgeous rose if you say your Hail Mary really well.

Of course it would be too much to expect you to say the whole fifteen mysteries every day, but do say at least five mysteries, and say them properly with love and devotion. This Rosary will be your little wreath of roses, your crown for Jesus and Mary. Please pay attention to every word I have said—and listen carefully to a true story that I want to tell you, and that I would like you to remember.

Two girls (two little sisters) were saying the Rosary very nicely and devoutly in front of their home. A beautiful Lady suddenly appeared, walked towards the younger—who was only about six or seven—took her by the hand, and led her away. Her elder sister was very startled and looked for the little girl everywhere. At last still not having found her, she went home and heartbrokenly told her parents that her sister had been kidnapped. For three whole days the poor father and mother sought the child but could not find her.

At the end of the third day they found her at the front door looking extremely happy and pleased. Naturally they asked her where on earth she had been, and she told them that the Lady to whom she had been saying her Rosary had taken her to a lovely place where she had given her delicious things to eat. She said that the Lady had also given her a Baby Boy to hold, that He was very beautiful and that she had kissed Him over and over again.

The father and mother, who had been converted to the Catholic Faith only a short time before, sent at once for the Jesuit Father who had instructed them for their reception into the Church and who had also taught them devotion to the Most Holy Rosary. They told him everything that had happened and it was this priest himself who told me this story. It all took place in Paraguay.

So, dear children imitate these little girls and say your Rosary every day as they always did. If you do this you will earn the right to go to Heaven to see Jesus and Mary. If it is not their wish that you should see them in this life, at any rate after you die you will see them for all eternity. Amen. So be it.

Therefore let all men, the learned and the ignorant, the just and the sinners, the great and the small praise and honor

Jesus and Mary, night and day, by saying the Most Holy Rosary. "Salute Mary who hath labored much among you." (*Rom.* 16:6).

PART I

WHAT THE ROSARY IS

First Rose

The Prayers of the Rosary

THE ROSARY is made up of two things: mental prayer and vocal prayer. In the Holy Rosary mental prayer is none other than meditation of the chief mysteries of the life, death and glory of Jesus Christ and of His Blessed Mother. Vocal prayer consists in saying fifteen decades of the Hail Mary, each decade headed by an Our Father, while at the same time meditating on and contemplating the fifteen principal virtues which Jesus and Mary practiced in the fifteen mysteries of the Holy Rosary.

In the first five decades we must honor the five Joyous Mysteries and meditate on them; in the second five decades the Sorrowful Mysteries and in the third group of five, the Glorious Mysteries. So the Rosary is a blessed blending of mental and vocal prayer by which we honor and learn to imitate the mysteries and the virtues of the life, death, Passion and glory of Jesus and Mary.

Second Rose

SINCE the Holy Rosary is composed, principally and in substance, of the Prayer of Christ and the Angelic Salutation, that is, the Our Father and the Hail Mary, it was without doubt the first prayer and the first devotion of the faithful and has been in use all through the centuries, from the time of the Apostles and disciples down to the present.

But it was only in the year 1214, however, that Holy Mother Church received the Rosary in its present form and according to the method we use today. It was given to the Church by Saint Dominic who had received it from the Blessed Virgin as a powerful means of converting the Albigensians and other sinners.

I will tell you the story of how he received it, which is found in the very well-known book *De Dignitate Psalterii* by Blessed Alan de la Roche.[1] Saint Dominic, seeing that the gravity of people's sins was hindering the conversion of the Albigensians, withdrew into a forest near Toulouse where he prayed unceasingly for three days and three nights. During this time he did nothing but weep and do harsh penances in order to appease the anger of Almighty God. He used his discipline so much that his body was lacerated, and finally he fell into a coma.

At this point Our Lady appeared to him, accompanied by three Angels, and she said:

"Dear Dominic, do you know which weapon the Blessed Trinity wants to use to reform the world?"

"Oh, my Lady," answered Saint Dominic, "you know far better than I do because next to your Son Jesus Christ you have always been the chief instrument of our salvation."

Then Our Lady replied:

"I want you to know that, in this kind of warfare, the bat-

---

1. *De Dignitate Psalterii.* The importance and Beauty of the Holy Rosary, by Blessed Alan de la Roche, O.P., French Dominican Father and Apostle of the Holy Rosary.

tering ram has always been the Angelic Psalter which is the foundation stone of the New Testament. Therefore if you want to reach these hardened souls and win them over to God, preach my Psalter."

So he arose, comforted, and burning with zeal for the conversion of the people in that district he made straight for the Cathedral. At once, unseen Angels rang the bells to gather the people together and Saint Dominic began to preach.

At the very beginning of his sermon an appalling storm broke out, the earth shook, the sun was darkened, and there was so much thunder and lightning that all were very much afraid. Even greater was their fear when looking at a picture of Our Lady exposed in a prominent place they saw her raise her arms to Heaven three times to call down God's vengeance upon them if they failed to be converted, to amend their lives, and seek the protection of the Holy Mother of God.

God wished, by means of these supernatural phenomena, to spread the new devotion of the Holy Rosary and to make it more widely known.

At last, at the prayer of Saint Dominic, the storm came to an end, and he went on preaching. So fervently and compellingly did he explain the importance and value of the Holy Rosary that almost all the people of Toulouse embraced it and renounced their false beliefs. In a very short time a great improvement was seen in the town; people began leading Christian lives and gave up their former bad habits.

Third Rose

THIS MIRACULOUS WAY in which the devotion to the Holy Rosary was established is something of a parallel to the way in which Almighty God gave His law to the world on Mount Sinai and obviously proves its value and importance.

Inspired by the Holy Ghost, instructed by the Blessed Virgin as well as by his own experience, Saint Dominic preached the Holy Rosary for the rest of his life. He preached it by his example as well as by his sermons, in cities and in country places, to people of high station and low, before scholars and the uneducated, to Catholics and to heretics.

The Holy Rosary which he said every day was his preparation for every sermon and his little tryst with Our Lady immediately after preaching.

One day he had to preach at Notre Dame in Paris, and it happened to be the feast of St. John the Evangelist. He was in a little chapel behind the high altar prayerfully preparing his sermon by saying the Rosary, as he always did, when Our Lady appeared to him and said:

"Dominic, even though what you have planned to say may be very good, I am bringing you a much better sermon."

Saint Dominic took in his hands the book Our Lady proffered, read the sermon carefully and when he had understood it and meditated on it, he gave thanks to the Blessed Mother.

When the time came, he went up into the pulpit and, in spite of the feast day, made no mention of Saint John other than to say that he had been found worthy to be the guardian of the Queen of Heaven. The congregation was made up of theologians and other eminent people who were used to hearing unusual and polished discourses; but Saint Dominic told them that it was not his wish to give them a learned discourse, wise in the eyes of the world, but that he would speak in the simplicity of the Holy Spirit and with His forcefulness.

So he began preaching the Holy Rosary and explained the Hail Mary word by word as he would to a group of children and used the very simple illustrations which were in the book Our Lady had given him.

Carthagena, the great scholar, quoting Blessed Alan de la Roche in *De Dignitate Psalterii,* describes how this took place:

"Blessed Alan writes that one day Father Dominic said to him in a vision: 'My son, it is good to preach; but there is always a danger of looking for praise rather than the salvation of souls. Listen carefully to what happened to me in Paris so that you may be on guard against this kind of mistake: I was to preach in the great church dedicated to the Blessed Virgin Mary and I was particularly anxious to give a brilliant sermon, not out of pride, but because of the high intellectual stature of the congregation.

'An hour before the time I had to preach, I was recollectedly saying my Rosary—as I always did before giving a sermon—when I fell into ecstasy. I saw my beloved friend the Mother of God coming towards me with a book in her hand. "Dominic," she said, "your sermon for today may be very good indeed, but no matter how good it is I have brought you one that is very much better."

'Of course I was overjoyed, took the book and read every word of it. Just as Our Lady had said, I found exactly the right things to say in my sermon, so I thanked her with all my heart.

'When it was time to begin, I saw that the University of Paris had turned out in full force as well as a large number of noblemen. They had all seen and heard of the great things that the good Lord had been doing through me. So I went up into the pulpit.

'It was the feast of Saint John the Apostle but all I said about him was that he had been found worthy to be the guardian of the Queen of Heaven. Then I addressed the congregation:

' "My Lords and illustrious Doctors of the University, you are accustomed to hearing learned sermons suited to your aesthetic tastes. Now I do not want to speak to you in the scholarly language of human wisdom but, on the contrary, to show you the Spirit of God and His Greatness.' "

Here ends the quotation from Blessed Alan, after which Carthagena goes on to say in his own words:

"Then Saint Dominic explained the Angelic Salutation to them, using simple comparisons and examples from everyday life."

Blessed Alan, according to Carthagena, mentioned several other times when Our Lord and Our Lady appeared to Saint Dominic to urge and inspire him to preach the Rosary more and more in order to wipe out sin and to convert sinners and heretics.

In another passage Carthagena says:

"Blessed Alan said Our Lady revealed to him that after she had appeared to Saint Dominic, her Blessed Son appeared to him and said:

'Dominic, I rejoice to see that you are not relying upon your own wisdom and that, rather than seek the empty praise of men, you are working with great humility for the salvation of souls.

'But many priests want to preach thunderously against the worst kinds of sin at the very outset, failing to realize that before a sick person is given bitter medicine he needs to be prepared by being put in the right frame of mind to really benefit by it.

'This is why, before doing anything else, priests should try to kindle a love of prayer in people's hearts and especially a love of my Angelic Psalter. If only they would all start saying it and would really persevere, God, in His mercy, could hardly refuse to give them His grace. So I want you to preach my Rosary.' "

In another place Blessed Alan says:

"All priests say a Hail Mary with the faithful before preaching, to ask for God's grace. They do this because of a revelation that Saint Dominic had from Our Lady. 'My son,' she said one day 'do not be surprised that your sermons fail to bear the results you had hoped for. You are trying to cultivate a piece of ground which has not had any rain. Now when Almighty God planned to renew the face of the earth He started by sending down rain from heaven— and this was the Angelic Salutation. In this way God made over the world.

'So when you give a sermon, urge people to say my Rosary, and in this way your words will bear much fruit for souls.'

"Saint Dominic lost no time in obeying, and from then on he exerted great influence by his sermons."

This last quotation is from the *Book of Miracles of the Holy Rosary* (written in Italian) and it is also to be found in Justin's works (143d Sermon).

I have been very glad to quote these well-known authors word for word in the original Latin[1] for benefit of any priests or other learned people who might otherwise have doubts as to the marvelous power of the Holy Rosary.

As long as priests followed Saint Dominic's example and preached devotion to the Holy Rosary, piety and fervor thrived throughout the Christian world and in those religious Orders which were devoted to the Rosary. But since people have neglected this gift from Heaven, all kinds of sin and disorder have spread far and wide.

---

1. We have omitted the Latin quotations so as not to encumber the text. English translations have been given above.

Fourth Rose

Blessed Alan de la Roche

A LL THINGS, even the holiest, are subject to change, especially when they are dependent on man's free will. It is hardly to be wondered at, then, that the Confraternity of the Holy Rosary only retained its first fervor for one century after it was instituted by Saint Dominic. After this, it was like a thing buried and forgotten.

Doubtless, too, the wicked scheming and jealousy of the devil were largely responsible for getting people to neglect the Holy Rosary, and thus block the flow of God's grace which it had drawn down upon the world.

Thus, in 1349, God punished the whole of Europe and sent the most terrible plague that had ever been known into every land. It started first in the east and spread throughout Italy, Germany, France, Poland and Hungary, bringing desolation wherever it came—for out of a hundred men hardly one lived to tell the tale. Big towns, little towns, villages and monasteries were almost completely deserted during the three years that the epidemic lasted.

This scourge of God was quickly followed by two others: the heresy of the Flagellantes and a tragic schism in 1376.

Later on when these trials were over, thanks to the mercy of God, Our Lady told Blessed Alan to revive the ancient Confraternity of the Most Holy Rosary. Blessed Alan was one of the Dominican Fathers from the monastery at Dinan, in Brittany. He was an eminent theologian and was famous for his sermons. Our Lady chose him because, since the Confraternity had originally been started in this province, it was most fitting that a Dominican from the very same province should have the honor of re-establishing it.

Blessed Alan began this great work in 1460 after a special warning from Our Lord. This is how he received His urgent message, as he tells it himself:

One day when he was saying Mass, Our Lord, Who

wished to spur him on to preach the Holy Rosary, spoke to him in the Sacred Host: "How can you crucify Me again so soon?" Jesus said. "What did You say, Lord?" asked Blessed Alan, horrified. "You crucified Me once before by your sins," answered Jesus, "and I would willingly be crucified again rather than have My Father offended by the sins you used to commit. You are crucifying Me again now because you have all the learning and understanding that you need to preach My Mother's Rosary, and you are not doing so. If you only did this you could teach many souls the right path and lead them away from sin—but you are not doing it and so you yourself are guilty of the sins that they commit."

This terrible reproach made Blessed Alan solemnly resolve to preach the Rosary unceasingly.

Our Lady too spoke to him one day to inspire him to preach the Holy Rosary more and more:

"You were a great sinner in your youth," she said, "but I obtained the grace of your conversion from my Son. Had such a thing been possible I would have liked to have gone through all kinds of suffering to save you because converted sinners are a glory to me. And I would have done this also to make you worthy of preaching my Rosary far and wide."

Saint Dominic appeared to Blessed Alan as well and told him of the great results of his ministry: he had preached the Holy Rosary unceasingly, his sermons had borne great fruit and many people had been converted during his missions. He said to Blessed Alan:

"See the wonderful results I have had through preaching the Holy Rosary! You and all those who love Our Lady ought to do the same so that, by means of this holy practice of the Rosary, you may draw all people to the real science of the virtues."

Briefly, then, this is the history of how Saint Dominic established the Holy Rosary and of how Blessed Alan de la Roche restored it.

Fifth Rose

S TRICTLY SPEAKING, there can be only one kind of Confraternity of the Rosary—one whose members agree to say the entire Rosary of one hundred and fifty Hail Marys every day. However, considering the fervor of those who say it, we may distinguish three kinds: Ordinary membership which entails saying the complete Rosary once a week; Perpetual membership which requires it be said only once a year; Daily membership which obliges one to say it all every day, that is, the fifteen decades made up of one hundred and fifty Hail Marys.

None of these Rosary memberships binds under pain of sin. It is not even a venial sin to fail in this duty because such an undertaking is entirely voluntary and supererogatory. Needless to say, people should not join the Confraternity if they do not intend to fulfill their obligation by saying the Rosary as often as is required, without, however, neglecting the duties of their state in life.

So whenever the Rosary clashes with a duty of one's state in life, holy as the Rosary is, one must give preference to the duty to be performed. Similarly, sick people are not obliged to say the whole Rosary or even part of it if this effort might tire them and make them worse.

If you have been unable to say it because of some duty required by obedience or because you genuinely forgot, or because of some urgent necessity, you have not committed even a venial sin. You will then receive the benefits of the Confraternity just the same, sharing in the graces and merits of your brothers and sisters in the Holy Rosary who are saying it throughout the world.

And, my dear Catholic people, even if you fail to say your Rosary out of sheer carelessness or laziness, as long as you do not have any formal contempt for it, you do not sin, absolutely speaking—but in this case you forfeit your participation in the prayers, good works and merits of the Confraternity. Moreover, because you have not been faithful in things that are little and of supererogation, almost without knowing it you may fall into the habit of neglecting big things such as those duties which bind under pain of sin. For—"He that contemneth small things, shall fall by little and little." (*Ecclus.* 19:1).

Sixth Rose

Mary's Psalter

EVER SINCE Saint Dominic established the devotion to the Holy Rosary up until the time when Blessed Alan de la Roche re-established it in 1460 it has always been called the Psalter of Jesus and Mary. This is because it has the same number of Angelic Salutations as there are psalms in the Book of the Psalms of David. Since simple and uneducated people are not able to say the Psalms of David the Rosary is held to be just as fruitful for them as David's Psalter is for others.

But the Rosary can be considered to be even more valuable than the latter for three reasons:

1. Firstly, because the Angelic Psalter bears a nobler fruit, that of the Word Incarnate, whereas David's Psalter only prophesies His coming;
2. Secondly, just as the real thing is more important than its prefiguration and as the body is more than its shadow, in the same way the Psalter of Our Lady is greater than David's Psalter which did no more than prefigure it;
3. And thirdly, because Our Lady's Psalter (or the Rosary made up of the Our Father and Hail Mary) is the direct work of the Most Blessed Trinity and was not made through a human instrument.

Our Lady's Psalter or Rosary is divided up into three parts

of five decades each, for the following special reasons:

1. To honor the three Persons of the Most Blessed Trinity;
2. To honor the life, death and glory of Jesus Christ;
3. To imitate the Church Triumphant, to help the members of the Church Militant and to lessen the pains of the Church Suffering;
4. To imitate the three groups into which the Psalms are divided:
   a) The first being for the purgative life,
   b) the second for the illuminative life,
   c) and the third for the unitive life;
5. And, finally, to give us graces in abundance during our lifetime, peace at death, and glory in eternity.

Seventh Rose

Crown of Roses

EVER SINCE Blessed Alan de la Roche re-established this devotion the voice of the people, which is the voice of God, called it the Rosary. The word Rosary means "Crown of Roses," that is to say that every time people say the Rosary devoutly they place a crown of one hundred and fifty-three white roses and sixteen red roses upon the heads of Jesus and Mary. Being heavenly flowers these roses will never fade or lose their exquisite beauty.

Our Lady has shown her thorough approval of the name Rosary; she has revealed to several people that each time they say a Hail Mary they are giving her a beautiful rose and that each complete Rosary makes her a crown of roses.

The well-known Jesuit, Brother Alphonsus Rodriguez, used to say his Rosary with such fervor that he often saw a red rose come out of his mouth at each Our Father and a white rose at each Hail Mary. The red and white roses were equal in beauty and fragrance, the only difference being in their color.

The chronicles of Saint Francis tell of a young friar who had the praiseworthy habit of saying the Crown of Our Lady (the Rosary) every day before dinner. One day for some reason or other he did not manage to say it. The refectory bell had already been rung when he asked the Superior to allow him to say it before coming to the table, and having obtained the permission he withdrew to his cell to pray.

After he had been gone a long time the Superior sent another Friar to fetch him, and he found him in his room bathed in a heavenly light facing Our Lady who had two Angels with her. Beautiful roses kept issuing from his mouth at each Hail Mary; the Angels took them one by one, placing them on Our Lady's head, and she smilingly accepted them.

Finally two other friars who had been sent to find out what had happened to the first two saw the same lovely scene, and Our Lady did not go away until the whole Rosary had been said.

So the complete Rosary is a large crown of roses and the Rosary of five decades is a little wreath of flowers or a small crown of heavenly roses which we place on the heads of Jesus and Mary. The rose is the queen of flowers, and so the Rosary is the rose of all devotions and it is therefore the most important one.

Eighth Rose

Marvels of the Rosary

IT WOULD hardly be possible for me to put into words how much Our Lady thinks of the Holy Rosary and of how she vastly prefers it to all other devotions. Neither can I sufficiently express how highly she rewards those who work to preach the devotion, to establish it and spread it, nor on the other hand how firmly she punishes those who work against it.

All during life, Saint Dominic had nothing more at heart than to praise Our Lady, to preach her greatness and to inspire everybody to honor her by saying her Rosary. As a reward he received countless graces from her; exercising her great power as Queen of Heaven she crowned his labors with many miracles and prodigies. Almighty God always granted him what he asked through Our Lady. The greatest honor of all was that she helped him crush the Albigensian heresy and made him the founder and patriarch of a great religious order.

As for Blessed Alan de la Roche who restored the devotion to the Rosary, he received many privileges from Our Lady; she graciously appeared to him several times to teach him how to work out his salvation, to become a good priest and perfect religious, and how to pattern himself on Our Lord.

He used to be horribly tempted and persecuted by devils, and then deep sadness would fall upon him and sometimes he used to be near to despair—but Our Lady always comforted him by her sweet presence which banished the clouds of darkness from his soul.

She taught him how to say the Rosary, explaining its value and the fruits to be gained by it and gave him a great and glorious privilege: the honor of being called her new spouse. As a token of her chaste love for him she placed a ring upon his finger and a necklace made of her own hair about his neck and gave him a Rosary.

Father Triteme, Carthagena and Martin of Navarre (both very learned men) and others as well have spoken of him in terms of the highest praise. Blessed Alan died at Zunolle in Flanders September 8th, 1475, after having brought over one hundred thousand people into the Confraternity.

Blessed Thomas of Saint John was well known for his sermons on the Most Holy Rosary, and the devil, jealous of the success he had with souls, tortured him so much that he fell ill and was sick so long that the doctors gave him up. One night when he really thought that he was dying, the devil appeared to him in the most horrible form imaginable. There was a picture of Our Lady near his bed; he looked at it and cried with all his heart and soul and strength: "Help me, save me, my sweet, sweet Mother!" No sooner had he said this than the picture seemed to come alive and Our Lady put out her hand, took him by the arm and said:

"Do not be afraid, Thomas my son, here I am and I am going to save you: get up now and go on preaching my Rosary as you used to do. I promise to shield you from your enemies."

When Our Lady said this the devil fled and Blessed Thomas got up, finding that he was in perfect health. He then thanked the Blessed Mother with tears of joy. He resumed his Rosary apostolate and his sermons were marvelously successful.

Our Lady blesses not only those who preach her Rosary, but she highly rewards all those who get others to say it by their example.

Alphonsus, King of Leon and Galicia, very much wanted all his servants to honor the Blessed Virgin by saying the Rosary. So he used to hang a large rosary on his belt and always wore it, but unfortunately never said it himself. Nevertheless his wearing it encouraged his courtiers to say the Rosary very devoutly.

One day the King fell seriously ill and when he was given up for dead he found himself, in a vision, before the judgment seat of Our Lord. Many devils were there accusing him of all the sins he had committed and Our Lord as Sovereign Judge was just about to condemn him to Hell when Our Lady appeared to intercede for him. She called for a pair of scales and had his sins placed in one of the balances whereas she put the rosary that he had always worn on the other scale, together with all the Rosaries that had been said because of his example. It was found that the Rosaries weighed more than his sins.

Looking at him with great kindness Our Lady said: "As a reward for this little honor that you paid me in wearing my Rosary, I have obtained a great grace for you from my Son.

Your life will be spared for a few more years. See that you spend these years wisely, and do penance."

When the King regained consciousness be cried out: "Blessed be the Rosary of the Most Holy Virgin Mary, by which I have been delivered from eternal damnation!"

After he had recovered his health he spent the rest of his life in spreading devotion to the Holy Rosary and said it faithfully every day.

People who love the Blessed Virgin ought to follow the example of King Alphonsus and that of the saints whom I have mentioned so that they too may win other souls for the Confraternity of the Holy Rosary. They will then receive great graces on earth and eternal life later on. "They that explain me shall have life everlasting." (*Ecclus.* 24:31).

Ninth Rose

Enemies

IT IS VERY WICKED indeed and unfair to other souls to hinder the progress of the Confraternity of the Holy Rosary. Almighty God has severely punished many of those who have been so benighted as to scorn the Confraternity and who have sought to destroy it.

Even though God has set His seal of approval on the Holy Rosary by many miracles, and in spite of the Papal Bulls that have been written approving it, there are only too many people who are against the Holy Rosary today. These freethinkers and those who scorn religion either condemn the Rosary or try to turn others away from it.

It is easy to see that they have absorbed the poison of Hell and that they are inspired by the devil—for nobody can condemn devotion to the Holy Rosary without condemning all that is most holy in the Catholic Faith, such as the Lord's Prayer, the Angelic Salutation and the mysteries of the life, death and glory of Jesus Christ and of His Holy Mother.

These freethinkers who cannot bear others to say the Rosary often fall into a really heretical state of mind without even realizing it and some to hate the Rosary and its holy mysteries.

To have a loathing for confraternities is to fall away from God and true piety, for Our Lord Himself has told us that He is always in the midst of those who are gathered together in His name. No good Catholic should forget the many great indulgences which Holy Mother Church has granted to Confraternities. Finally, to dissuade others from joining the Rosary Confraternity is to be an enemy of souls because the Rosary is a sure means of curing oneself of sin and of embracing a Christian life.

Saint Bonaventure said (in his Psalter) that whoever neglected Our Lady would perish in his sins and would be damned: "He who neglects her will die in his sins." If such is the penalty for neglecting her, what must be the punishment in store for those who actually turn others away from their devotions!

Tenth Rose

Miracles

WHILE SAINT DOMINIC was preaching the Rosary in Carcassone, a heretic made fun of the miracles and the fifteen mysteries of the Holy Rosary, and this prevented other heretics from being converted. As a punishment God suffered fifteen thousand devils to enter the man's body.

His parents took him to Father Dominic to be delivered from the evil spirits. He started to pray and begged everyone who was there to say the Rosary out loud with him, and at each Hail Mary Our Lady drove one hundred devils out of the heretic's body and they came out in the form of red hot coals.

After he had been delivered he abjured his former errors, was converted and joined the Rosary Confraternity. Several of his associates did the same, having been greatly moved by his punishment and by the power of the Rosary.

The learned Franciscan, Carthagena, as well as several other authors, says that an extraordinary event took place in 1482: The Venerable James Sprenger and other religious of his order were zealously working to re-establish devotion to the Holy Rosary and also to erect a Confraternity in the city of Cologne.

Unfortunately two priests who were famous for their preaching ability were jealous of the great influence they were exerting through preaching the Rosary. So these two Fathers spoke against this devotion whenever they had a chance, and as they were very eloquent and had a great reputation they persuaded many people not to join the Confraternity.

One of them, bound and determined to achieve his wicked end, wrote a special sermon against the Rosary and planned to give it the following Sunday. But when it came time for the sermon he never appeared and, after a certain amount of waiting somebody went to fetch him. He was found dead, and evidently had died all alone without any one to help him and without seeing a priest.

After convincing himself that death had been due to natural causes, the other priest decided to carry out his friend's plan and to give a similar sermon on another day. In this way he hoped to put an end to the Confraternity of the Rosary. However, when the day came for him to preach and it was time to give the sermon God punished him by striking him down with paralysis which deprived him both of the use of his limbs and of his power of speech.

At last he admitted his sin and likewise that of his friend and immediately, in his heart of hearts, he silently besought Our Lady to help him. He promised her that if she would only cure him he would preach the Holy Rosary with as much zeal as that with which he had formerly fought against it. For this end he implored her to restore his health and speech which she did, and finding himself instantaneously cured he rose up like another Saul, a persecutor turned defender of the Holy Rosary. He publicly acknowledged his former error and ever after preached the wonders of the Most Holy Rosary with great zeal and eloquence.

I am quite sure that freethinkers and ultra-critical people of today will question the truth of the stories in this little book, in the very same way that they have always questioned most things, but all that I have done has been to copy them from very good contemporary writers and also, in part, from a book that was written only a short time ago: *The Mystical Rose Tree,* by the Reverend Antonin Thomas, O.P.

Everyone knows that there are three different kinds of faith by which we believe different kinds of stories:

To stories of Holy Scripture we owe *divine faith*;

To stories concerning other than religious subjects, which do not militate against common sense and which are written by trustworthy authors, we pay the tribute of *human faith*; whereas

To stories about holy subjects which are told by good authors and are not in the slightest degree contrary to reason, faith or morals (even though they may sometimes deal with happenings which are above the ordinary run of events) we pay the tribute of *pious faith.*

I agree that we must be neither too credulous nor too critical and that we should remember that *"virtue takes the middle course"*—keeping a happy medium in all things in order to find just where truth and virtue lie. But on the other hand I know equally well that charity easily leads us to believe all that is not contrary to faith or morals: "Charity . . . believeth all things;" (*1 Cor.* 13:7) in the same way pride induces us to doubt even well authenticated stories on the plea that they are not to be found in the Bible.

This is one of the devil's traps; heretics of the past who denied Tradition have fallen into it and over-critical people of today are falling into it too without even realizing it.

People of this kind refuse to believe what they do not understand or what is not to their liking, simply because of their own spirit of pride and independence.

Eleventh Rose

The Creed

THE CREED or the Symbol of the Apostles which is said on the crucifix of the Rosary is a holy summary of all Christian truths. It is a prayer that has great merit because faith is the root, foundation and beginning of all Christian virtues, of all eternal virtues and also of all prayers that are pleasing to Almighty God. "He that cometh to God, must believe . . ." (*Heb.* 11:6). Whosoever wishes to come to God must first of all believe and the greater his faith the more merit his prayer will have, the more powerful it will be, and the more it will glorify God.

I shall not take time here to explain the Creed word for word but I cannot resist saying that the first few words "I believe in God" are marvelously effective as a means of sanctifying our souls and of putting devils to rout, because these three words contain the acts of the three theological virtues of faith, hope and charity.

It was by saying *I believe in God* that the saints overcame temptations, especially those against faith, hope or charity—whether they came during their lifetime or at their death. They were also the last words of St. Peter, Martyr;[1] a heretic had cleft his head in two by a cruel blow of his sword and St. Peter was almost at his last gasp, but he somehow managed to trace these words in the sand with his finger before he died.

---

1. Saint Peter of Verona, O.P. 1206-1253, was a Dominican priest who fought heresy courageously and zealously. He had the honor of receiving the habit from the hands of Saint Dominic himself. He was appointed Inquisitor for Lombardy, and it was in discharging his duties that he gave his life for the Faith.

The Holy Rosary contains many mysteries of Jesus and Mary and since faith is the only key which opens up these mysteries for us we must begin the Rosary by saying the Creed very devoutly, and the stronger our faith the more merit our Rosary will have.

This faith must be lively and informed by charity; in other words, to recite properly the Rosary, it is necessary to be in God's grace, or at least in quest of it. This faith must be strong and constant, that is, one must not be looking for sensible devotion and spiritual consolation in the recitation of the Rosary; nor should one give it up because his mind is flooded with countless involuntary distractions or one experiences a strange distaste in the soul and an almost continual and oppressive fatigue in the body. Neither feeling, nor consolation, nor sighs, nor transports, nor the continual attention of the imagination are needed; faith and good intentions are quite enough. "Faith alone suffices."[2]

Twelfth Rose

The Our Father

THE OUR FATHER or the Lord's prayer has great value—above all because of its Author Who is neither a man nor an angel but the King of angels and men, Our Lord and Savior Jesus Christ. Saint Cyprian says that it was fitting that our Savior by Whom we were reborn into the life of grace should also be our heavenly Master and should teach us how to pray.

The beautiful order, the tender forcefulness and the clarity of this divine prayer pay tribute to our divine Master's wisdom. It is a short prayer but can teach us so very much and it is well within the grasp of uneducated people, while scholars find it a continual source of meditation on the mysteries of our Faith.

---

2. From the Pange Lingua.

The Our Father contains all the duties we owe to God, the acts of all the virtues and the petitions for all our spiritual and corporal needs. Tertullian says that the Our Father is a summary of the New Testament. Thomas à Kempis says that it surpasses all the desires of all the Saints; that it is a condensation of all the beautiful sayings of all the Psalms and Canticles; that in it we ask God for everything that we need; that by it we praise Him in the very best way; that by it we lift up our souls from earth to heaven and unite them with God.

Saint John Chrysostom says that we cannot be our Master's disciples unless we pray as He did and in the way that He showed us. Moreover God the Father listens more willingly to the Prayer that we have learned from His Son rather than those of our own making which have all our human limitations.

We should say the Our Father with the certitude that the eternal Father will hear it because it is the prayer of His Son Whom He always hears and we are His members. God will surely grant our petitions made through the Lord's Prayer because it is impossible to imagine that such a good Father could refuse a request couched in the language of so worthy a Son, reinforced by His merits, and made at His behest.

Saint Augustine says that whenever we say the Our Father devoutly our venial sins are forgiven. The just man falls seven times a day, but in the Lord's Prayer he will find seven petitions which will both help him to avoid downfalls and will protect him from his spiritual enemies. Our Lord, knowing how weak and helpless we are, and how many difficulties we get into, made His Prayer short and easy to say, so that if we say it devoutly and often we can be sure that Almighty God will quickly come to our aid.

I have a word for you, devout souls, who pay little attention to the prayer that the Son of God gave us Himself and asked us all to say: It is high time for you to change your way of thinking. You only like prayers that men have written—as though anybody, even the most inspired man in the whole world, could possibly know more about how we ought to pray than Jesus Christ Himself! You look for prayers in books written by other men almost as though you were ashamed of saying the prayer that Our Lord told us to say.

You have managed to convince yourself that the prayers in these books are for scholars and for rich people of the upper classes and that the Rosary is only for women and children and the lower classes. As if the prayers and praises which you have been reading were more beautiful and more pleasing to God than those which are to be found in the Lord's Prayer! It is a very dangerous temptation to lose interest in the prayer that Our Lord gave us and to take up prayers that men have written instead.

Not that I disapprove of prayers that the saints have written so as to encourage the faithful to praise God, but it is not to be endured that they should prefer the latter to the Prayer which was uttered by Wisdom Incarnate. If they ignore this Prayer it is just as though they pass up the spring to go after the brook and refusing the clear water, drink dirty water instead. Because the Rosary made up of the Lord's Prayer and the Angelic Salutation, is this clear and everflowing water which comes from the Fountain of Grace, whereas other prayers which they look for in books are nothing but tiny streams which spring from this fountain.

People who say Our Lord's Prayer carefully, weighing every word and meditating upon it, may indeed call themselves blessed for they find therein everything that they need or can wish for.

When we say this wonderful prayer we touch God's heart at the very outset by calling Him by the sweet name of Father—Our Father. He is the dearest of fathers: all-powerful in His creation, wonderful in the way He maintains the world, completely lovable in His Divine Providence— always good and infinitely so in the Redemption. We have God for our Father, so we are all brothers—and heaven is our homeland and our heritage. This should be more than enough to teach us to love God and our neighbor and to be detached from the things of this world.

So we ought to love our Heavenly Father and should say
to Him over and over again:

> *Our Father Who art in heaven,*
> Thou Who dost fill heaven and earth
> With the immensity of Thy Being,
> Thou Who art present everywhere—
> Thou Who art in the saints
> By Thy glory,
> In the damned
> By Thy Justice,
> In the good
> By Thy grace—
> And even in sinners
> By the patience
> With which Thou dost tolerate them—
> Grant we beseech Thee
> That we may always remember
> That we come from Thee;
> Grant that we may live
> As Thy true children ought to live—
> Grant that we may set our course
> Towards Thee
> And never swerve—
> Grant that we may use
> Our every power,
> Our hearts and souls and strength
> To tend towards Thee
> And THEE ALONE.

Hallowed be Thy name:

King David, the prophet, said that the name of the Lord is
holy and awe-inspiring, and Isaias that heaven is always
echoing with the praises of the Seraphim who unceasingly
praise the holiness of the Lord God of Hosts.

We ask here that all the world may learn to know and adore the attributes of our God Who is so great and so holy. We ask that He may be known, loved and adored by pagans, Turks, Jews, barbarians and by all infidels—that all men may serve and glorify Him by a living faith, a staunch hope, a burning charity and by renouncing all erroneous beliefs. This all adds up to say that we pray that all men may be holy, because our God Himself is all-holy.

Thy Kingdom come:

> Do Thou reign in our souls
> By Thy grace
> So that after death
> We may be found meet
> To reign with Thee
> In Thy Kingdom
> In perfect and unending bliss.
> Oh Lord we firmly believe
> In this happiness to come;
> We hope for and we expect it,
> Because God the Father
> Has promised it
> In His great goodness;
> It was purchased for us
> By the merits of God the Son
> And God the Holy Spirit
> He Who is the Light
> Has made it known to us.

Thy will be done on earth as it is in heaven:

As Tertullian says, this sentence does not in the least mean that we are afraid of people thwarting God's designs because nothing whatsoever can happen without Divine Providence having foreseen it and having made it fit into His plans beforehand. No obstruction in the whole world can possibly prevent the will of God from being carried out.

Rather, when we say *Thy will be done,* we ask God to make us humbly resigned to all that He has seen fit to send us in this life. We also ask Him to help us to do, in all things and at all times, His Holy will, made known to us by the commandments, promptly, lovingly and faithfully as the Saints and Angels do it in Heaven.

Give us this day our daily bread:

Our Lord taught us to ask God for everything that we need whether in the spiritual or temporal order. By asking for our *daily bread* we humbly admit our own poverty and insufficiency and pay tribute to our God, knowing that all temporal goods come from His Divine Providence.

When we say *bread* we ask for that which is just necessary to live; and, of course, this does not include luxuries.

We ask for this bread today *this day* which means that we are concerned only for the present, leaving the morrow in the hands of Providence.

And when we ask for our *daily bread* we recognize that we need God's help every day and that we are entirely dependent upon Him for His help and protection.

Forgive us our trespasses as we forgive those who trespass against us:

Every sin, say Saint Augustine and Tertullian, is a debt which we contract towards Almighty God, and His justice demands payment down to the very last farthing. Unfortunately we all have these sad debts.

No matter how many they may be we should go to God in all confidence and with true sorrow for our sins, saying "Our Father Who art in Heaven, forgive us our sins of thought and those of speech, forgive us our sins of commission and omission which make us infinitely guilty in the eyes of Thy Divine Justice.

"We dare to ask this because Thou art our loving and merciful Father and because we have forgotten those who have offended us, out of obedience to Thee and out of charity.

"Do not permit us, in spite of our infidelity to Thy graces, to give in to the temptations of the world, the devil and the flesh."

But deliver us from evil:

The evil of sin and also of temporal punishment and ever-lasting punishment which we know that we have rightly deserved.

Amen (So be it).

This word at the end of the Our Father is very consoling and Saint Jerome says that it is a sort of seal of approbation that Almighty God puts at the end of our petitions to assure us that He will grant our requests—very much as though He Himself were answering:
"Amen! May it be as you have asked, for verily you have obtained what you asked for." This is what is meant by the word "Amen."

Thirteenth Rose

The Our Father (Continued)

EACH WORD of the Lord's Prayer is a tribute we pay to the perfections of God. We honor His fertility by the name of Father:

> FATHER,
> Thou
> Who throughout eternity
> Dost beget a Son
> Who is God like Thee—
> Eternal, consubstantial with Thee
> WHO Is the very same essence

As Thee;
And is of like power
And goodness
And wisdom
As Thou art . . .
Father and Son
Who from Your mutual love
Produce the Holy Spirit
Who is God like unto You;
Three Persons
But one GOD.

Our Father—this means that He is the Father of mankind because He has created us and continues to sustain us, and because He has redeemed us. He is also the merciful Father of sinners, the Father Who is the friend of the just and the glorious Father of the blessed in Heaven.

When we say *Who art*, by these words we pay tribute to the infinity and immensity and fullness of God's essence. God is rightly called "He Who is" (*Ex.* 3:14); that is to say, He exists of necessity, essentially, and eternally, because He is the Being of beings and the cause of all beings. He possesses within Himself, in a supereminent degree, the perfections of all beings and He is in all of them by His essence, by His presence and by His power, but without being bounded by their limitations. We honor His sublimity and His glory and His majesty by the words *Who art in heaven*, that is to say, "Who is seated as on a throne, holding sway over all men by Thy justice."

When we say *hallowed be Thy name* we worship God's holiness; and we make obeisance to His Kingship and bow to the justice of His laws by the words *Thy Kingdom come*, praying that men will obey Him on earth as the Angels do in Heaven.

We show our trust in His Providence by asking for our *daily bread*, and we appeal to His mercy when we ask for the forgiveness of our sins.

We look to His great power when we beg Him *not to lead us into temptation,* and we show our faith in His goodness by our hope that He will *deliver us from evil.*

The Son of God has always glorified His Father by His works and He came into the world to teach men to give glory to Him. He showed men how to praise Him by this prayer which He taught us with His own lips. It is our duty, there-fore, to say it often—we should say it reverently and atten-tively and in the spirit in which Our Lord taught it.

Fourteenth Rose

The Our Father (Continued)

WE MAKE as many acts of the noblest Christian virtues as we pronounce words, when we recite attentively this divine prayer.

In saying *"Our Father Who art in heaven,"* we make acts of faith, adoration and humility. When we ask that *His name be hallowed* and glorified we show a burning zeal for His glory, and when we ask for the spread of His Kingdom we make an act of hope; by the wish that *His will be done on earth as it is in heaven,* we show a spirit of perfect obedience.

In asking for our *daily bread* we practice poverty of spirit and detachment from worldly goods. When we beg Him to *forgive us our sins* we make an act of sorrow for them. By *forgiving those who have trespassed against us* we give proof of the virtue of mercy in its highest degree.

Through asking God's *help in all our temptations*, we make acts of humility, prudence and fortitude. As we wait for Him to *deliver us from evil* we exercise the virtue of patience.

Finally, while asking for all these things—not for our-selves alone but also for our neighbor and for all members of the Church—we are carrying out our duty as true children of God, we are imitating Him in His love which embraces all men and we are keeping the commandment of love of neighbor.

If we mean in our hearts what we say with our lips and if our intentions are not at variance with those expressed in the Lord's Prayer, then, by reciting this prayer, we hate all sin and we observe all of God's laws. For whenever we think that God is in Heaven—infinitely removed from us by the greatness of His majesty—as we place ourselves in His presence we should be filled with overwhelming reverence. Then the fear of the Lord will chase away all pride and we will bow down before God in our utter nothingness.

When we say the name *Father* and remember that we owe our existence to God by the means of our parents and even our knowledge to our teachers who hold the place and are the living images of God, then we cannot help paying them honor and respect, or, to be more exact, honoring God in them. Nothing then, too, would be farther from our thoughts than to be disrespectful to them or hurt them.

We are never farther from blaspheming than when we pray that the *Holy Name of God may be glorified*. If we really look upon the Kingdom of God as our heritage we cannot possibly be attached to the things of this world.

If we sincerely ask God that our neighbor may have the very same blessings that we ourselves stand in need of, it goes without saying that we will give up all hatred, quarreling and jealousy. And of course if we ask God each day for our *daily bread* we shall learn to hate gluttony and lasciviousness which thrive in rich surroundings.

While sincerely asking God *to forgive us as we forgive those who trespass against us* we no longer give way to anger and thoughts of getting even—we return good for evil and really love our enemies.

To ask God to *save us from falling into sin* when we are tempted is to give proof that we are fighting laziness and that we are genuinely seeking means to root out vicious habits and to work out our salvation.

To pray God to *deliver us from evil* is to fear His justice and this will give us true happiness. For since the fear of God is the beginning of wisdom, it is through the virtue of the fear of God that men avoid sin.

Fifteenth Rose

The Hail Mary

THE ANGELIC SALUTATION is so heavenly and so beyond us in its depth of meaning that Blessed Alan de la Roche held that no mere creature could ever possibly understand it, and that only Our Lord and Savior Jesus Christ Who was born of the Blessed Virgin Mary can really explain it.

Its enormous value is due first of all to Our Lady to whom it was addressed, to the purpose of the Incarnation of the Word for which reason this prayer was brought from Heaven, and also to the Archangel Gabriel who was the first ever to say it.

The Angelic Salutation is a most concise summary of all that Catholic theology teaches about the Blessed Virgin. It is divided into two parts, that of praise and petition: the first shows all that goes to make up Mary's greatness and the second all that we need to ask her for and all that we may expect to receive through her goodness.

The Most Blessed Trinity revealed the first part of it to us and the latter part was added by Saint Elizabeth who was inspired by the Holy Spirit. Holy Mother Church gave us the conclusion in the year 430 when she condemned the Nestorian heresy at the Council of Ephesus and defined that the Blessed Virgin is truly the Mother of God. At this time she ordered us to pray to Our Lady under this glorious title by saying:

"Holy Mary, Mother of God, pray for us sinners, now, and at the hour of our death."

The greatest event in the whole history of the world was the Incarnation of the Eternal Word by Whom the world was redeemed and peace was restored between God and men. Our Lady was chosen as His instrument for this tremendous event and it was put into effect when she was greeted with the Angelic Salutation. The Archangel Gabriel, one of the leading princes of the heavenly court, was chosen as ambassador to bear these glad tidings.

In the Angelic Salutation can be seen the faith and hope of the patriarchs, the prophets and the apostles. Furthermore it gives to martyrs their unswerving constancy and strength, it is the wisdom of the doctors of the Church, the perseverance of holy confessors and the life of all religious. (Blessed Alan de la Roche). It is also the new hymn of the law of grace, the joy of angels and men, and the hymn which terrifies devils and puts them to shame.

By the Angelic Salutation God became man, a virgin became the Mother of God, the souls of the just were delivered from Limbo, the empty thrones in heaven filled. In addition sin was forgiven, grace was given to us, sick people were made well, the dead were brought back to life, exiles were brought home, and the anger of the Most Blessed Trinity was appeased and men obtained eternal life.

Finally, the Angelic Salutation is a rainbow in the heavens, a sign of the mercy and grace which God has given to the world. (Blessed Alan da la Roche).

Sixteenth Rose

The Hail Mary—Beauty

EVEN THOUGH THERE IS nothing so great as the majesty of God and nothing so low as man insofar as he is a sinner, Almighty God does not despise our poor prayers. On the contrary, He is pleased when we sing His praises.

Saint Gabriel's greeting to Our Lady is one of the most

beautiful hymns which we can possibly sing to the glory of the Most High. "I will sing a new song to you." (*Ps.* 143:9). This new hymn which David foretold was to be sung at the coming of the Messias is none other than the Angelic Salutation.

There is an old hymn and a new hymn: the first is that which the Jews sang out of gratitude to God for creating them and maintaining them in existence—for delivering them from captivity and leading them safely through the Red Sea—for giving them manna to eat and for all His other blessings.

The new hymn is that which Christians sing in thanksgiving for the graces of the Incarnation and the Redemption. As these marvels were brought about by the Angelic Salutation, so also do we repeat the same salutation to thank the Most Blessed Trinity for His immeasurable goodness to us.

We praise God the Father because He so loved the world that He gave us His only Son as our Savior. We bless the Son because He deigned to leave Heaven and come down upon earth—because HE WAS MADE MAN and redeemed us. We glorify the Holy Spirit because He formed Our Lord's pure Body in Our Lady's Womb—this Body which was the Victim of our sins. In this spirit of deep thankfulness should we, then, always say the Hail Mary, making acts of faith, hope, love and thanksgiving for the priceless gift of salvation.

Although this new hymn is in praise of the Mother of God and is sung directly to her, nevertheless it greatly glorifies the Most Blessed Trinity because any homage that we pay Our Lady returns inevitably to God Who is the cause of all her virtues and perfections. When we honor Our Lady: God the Father is glorified because we are honoring the most perfect of His creatures; God the Son is glorified because we are praising His most pure Mother, and God the Holy Spirit is glorified because we are lost in admiration at the graces with which He has filled His Spouse.

When we praise and bless Our Lady by saying the Angelic

Salutation she always passes on these praises to Almighty God in the same way as she did when she was praised by Saint Elizabeth. The latter blessed her in her most elevated dignity as Mother of God and Our Lady immediately returned these praises to God by her beautiful Magnificat.

Just as the Angelic Salutation gives glory to the Blessed Trinity, it is also the very highest praise that we can give Our Lady.

One day when Saint Mechtilde was praying and was trying to think of some way in which she could express her love of the Blessed Mother better than she had done before, she fell into ecstasy. Our Lady appeared to her with the Angelic Salutation in flaming letters of gold upon her bosom and said to her: "My daughter, I want you to know that no one can please me more than by saying the salutation which the Most Adorable Trinity sent to me and by which He raised me to the dignity of Mother of God.

"By the word *Ave* (which is the name Eve, Eva), I learned that in His infinite power God had preserved me from all sin and its attendant misery which the first woman had been subject to.

"The name *Mary* which means 'lady of light' shows that God has filled me with wisdom and light, like a shining star, to light up heaven and earth.

"The words *full of grace* remind me that the Holy Spirit has showered so many graces upon me that I am able to give these graces in abundance to those who ask for them through me as Mediatrix.

"When people say *The Lord is with thee* they renew the indescribable joy that was mine when the Eternal Word became incarnate in my womb.

"When you say to me *blessed art thou among women* I praise Almighty God's divine mercy which lifted me to this exalted plane of happiness.

"And at the words *blessed is the fruit of thy womb, Jesus,* the whole of heaven rejoices with me to see my Son Jesus Christ adored and glorified for having saved mankind."

Seventeenth Rose

The Hail Mary—Fruits

B LESSED ALAN DE LA ROCHE who was so deeply devoted to the Blessed Virgin had many revelations from her and we know that be confirmed the truth of these revelations by a solemn oath. Three of them stand out with special emphasis: the first, that if people fail to say the Hail Mary (the Angelic Salutation which has saved the world) out of carelessness, or because they are lukewarm, or because they hate it, this is a sign that they will probably and indeed shortly be condemned to eternal punishment.

The second truth is that those who love this divine salutation bear the very special stamp of predestination.

The third is that those to whom God has given the signal grace of loving Our Lady and of serving her out of love must take very great care to continue to love and serve her until the time when she shall have had them placed in Heaven by her divine Son in the degree of glory which they have earned. (Blessed Alan, chapter XI, paragraph 2).

The heretics, all of whom are children of the devil and clearly bear the sign of God's reprobation, have a horror of the Hail Mary. They still say the Our Father but never the Hail Mary; they would rather wear a poisonous snake around their necks than wear a scapular or carry a rosary.

Among Catholics those who bear the mark of God's reprobation think but little of the Rosary (whether that of five decades or fifteen). They either fail to say it or only say it very quickly and in a lukewarm manner.

Even if I did not believe that which has been revealed to Blessed Alan de la Roche, even then my own experience would be enough to convince me of this terrible but consoling truth. I do not know, nor do I see clearly, how it can be that a devotion which seems to be so small can be the infallible sign of eternal salvation and how its absence can be the sign of God's eternal displeasure; nevertheless, nothing could possibly be more true.

In our own day we see that people who hold new doctrines that have been condemned by Holy Mother Church may have quite a bit of surface piety, but they scorn the Rosary, and often dissuade their acquaintances from saying it, by destroying their love of it and their faith in it. In doing this they make elaborate excuses which are plausible in the eyes of the world. They are very careful not to condemn the Rosary and the Scapular as the Calvinists do—but the way they set about attacking them is all the more deadly because it is the more cunning. I shall refer to it again later on.

My Hail Mary, my Rosary of fifteen or of five decades, is the prayer and the infallible touchstone by which I can tell those who are led by the Spirit of God from those who are deceived by the devil. I have known souls who seemed to soar like eagles to the heights by their sublime contemplation and who yet were pitifully led astray by the devil. I only found out how wrong they were when I learned that they scorned the Hail Mary and the Rosary which they considered as being far beneath them.

The Hail Mary is a blessed dew that falls from heaven upon the souls of the predestinate. It gives them a marvelous spiritual fertility so that they can grow in all virtues. The more the garden of the soul is watered by this prayer the more enlightened one's intellect becomes, the more zealous his heart, and the stronger his armor against his spiritual enemies.

The Hail Mary is a sharp and flaming shaft which, joined to the Word of God, gives the preacher the strength to pierce, move and convert the most hardened hearts even if he has little or no natural gift for preaching.

As I have already said, this was the great secret that Our Lady taught Saint Dominic and Blessed Alan so that they might convert heretics and sinners.

Saint Antoninus tells us that this is why many priests got into the habit of saying a Hail Mary at the beginning of their sermons.

Eighteenth Rose

The Hail Mary—Blessings

THIS HEAVENLY SALUTATION draws down upon us the blessings of Jesus and Mary in abundance, for it is an infallible truth that Jesus and Mary reward in a marvelous way those who glorify them. They repay us a hundredfold for the praises that we give them. "I love them that love me . . . that I may enrich them that love me and fill their treasures." (*Prov.* 8:17, 21). Jesus and Mary have always said: "We love those who love us; we enrich them and fill their treasuries to overflowing." "He who soweth in blessings, shall also reap blessings." (*Cor.* 9:6).

Now, if we say the Hail Mary properly, is not this a way to love, bless and glorify Jesus and Mary?

In each Hail Mary we bless both Jesus and Mary: "Blessed art thou among women, and blessed is the fruit of thy womb, Jesus."

By each Hail Mary we give Our Lady the same honor that God gave her when He sent the Archangel Gabriel to greet her for Him. How could anyone possibly think that Jesus and Mary, who often do good to those that curse them, could ever curse those that bless and honor them by the Hail Mary?

Both Saint Bernard and Saint Bonaventure say that the Queen of Heaven is certainly no less grateful and conscientious than gracious and well-mannered people of this world. Just as she excels in all other perfections, she surpasses us all in the virtue of gratitude; so she would never let us honor her with love and respect without repaying us one hundredfold. Saint Bonaventure says that Mary will greet us with grace if we greet her with the Hail Mary.

Who could possibly understand the graces and blessings which the greeting and tender regard of Our Lady effect in us? From the very first instant that Saint Elizabeth heard the greeting that the Mother of God gave her, she was filled with the Holy Spirit and the child in her womb leaped for joy. If we make ourselves worthy of the greeting and blessings of Our Lady we shall certainly be filled with graces and a flood of spiritual consolations will come down into our souls.

Nineteenth Rose

Happy Exchange

IT IS WRITTEN: "Give and it shall be given unto you." (*Luke* 6:38). To take Blessed Alan's illustration of this: "Supposing each day I give you one hundred and fifty diamonds, even if you were my enemy, would you not forgive me? Would you not treat me as a friend and give me all the graces that you were able to give? If you want to gain the riches of grace and of glory, salute the Blessed Virgin, honor your good Mother." "He that honoreth his mother (the Blessed Virgin) is as one that layeth up a treasure." (*Ecclus.* 3:5). So every day do give her at least fifty Hail Marys—for each one is worth fifteen precious stones and they please Our Lady far more than all the riches of this world put together.

And you can expect such great things from her generosity! She is our Mother and our friend. She is the empress of the universe and loves us more than all the mothers and queens of the world have ever loved any one human being. This is really so, for the charity of the Blessed Virgin far surpasses the natural love of all mankind and even of all the angels, as Saint Augustine says.

One day Saint Gertrude had a vision of Our Lord counting gold coins. She summoned the courage to ask Him what He was doing. He answered: "I am counting the Hail Marys that you have said; this is the money with which you can pay your way to Heaven."

The holy and learned Jesuit, Father Suarez, was so deeply aware of the value of the Angelic Salutation that he said that he would gladly give all his learning for the price of one Hail

Mary that had been said properly.

Blessed Alan de la Roche said: "Let everyone who loves you, oh most holy Mary, listen to this and drink it in:

> Whenever I say
> Hail Mary
> The court of heaven rejoices
> And the earth
> Is lost in wonderment.
> And I despise the world
> And my heart is brim-full
> Of the love of God
> When I say
> Hail Mary;
> All my fears
> Wilt and die
> And my passions are quelled
> If I say
> Hail Mary;
> Devotion grows
> Within me
> And sorrow for sin
> Awakens
> When I say
> Hail Mary.
> Hope is made strong
> In my breast
> And the dew of consolation
> Falls on my soul
> More and more—
> Because I say
> Hail Mary.
> And my spirit
> Rejoices
> And sorrow fades away
> When I say
> Hail Mary . . .

For the sweetness of this blessed salutation is so great that there are no words to explain it adequately, and even when its wonders have been sung, we still find it so full of mystery and so profound that its depths can never be plumbed. It has but few words but is exceeding rich in mystery; it is sweeter than honey and more precious than gold. We should often meditate upon it in our hearts and have it ever upon our lips so as to say it devoutly again and again."

Blessed Alan says that a nun who had always had great devotion to the Holy Rosary appeared after death to one of her sisters in religion and said to her: "If I were allowed to go back into my body, to have the chance of saying just one single Hail Mary—even if I said it quickly and without great fervor—I would gladly go through the sufferings that I had during my last illness all over again, in order to gain the merit of this prayer." (Blessed Alan de la Roche, *De Dignitate Psalterii,* Chapter LXIX). This is all the more compelling because she had been bedridden and had suffered agonizing pains for several years before she died.

Michel de Lisle, Bishop of Salubre, who was a disciple and co-worker of Blessed Alan's in the re-establishment of the Holy Rosary said that the Angelic Salutation is the remedy for all ills that we suffer as long as we say it devoutly in honor of Our Lady.

Twentieth Rose

The Hail Mary—Explanation

ARE YOU in the miserable state of sin? Then call on the divine[1] Mary and say to her: *Ave*, which means "I salute thee with the most profound respect, thou who art without sin" and she will deliver you from the evil of your sins.

Are you groping in the darkness of ignorance and error? Go to Mary and say to her: *Hail Mary*; which means "Hail thou who art bathed in the light of the Sun of Justice"—and she will give you some of her light.

Have you strayed from the path leading to Heaven? Then call on Mary, for her name means "Star of the Sea, the North Star which guides the ships of our souls during the voyage of this life," and she will guide you to the harbor of eternal salvation.

Are you in sorrow? Turn to Mary, for her name means also "Sea of Bitterness which has been filled with sharp pain in this world but which is now turned into a Sea of the Purest Joy in heaven," and she will turn your sorrow to joy and your afflictions into consolation.

Have you lost the state of grace? Praise and honor the numberless graces with which God has filled the Blessed Virgin and say to her: *Thou art full of grace* and filled with all the gifts of the Holy Spirit, and she will give you some of these graces.

Are you all alone, having lost God's protection? Pray to Mary, and say: "*The Lord is with thee*—and this union is far nobler and more intimate than that which He has with saints and the just—because thou art one with Him. He is thy Son

---

1. ". . . the word divine may be used without attributing the nature of divinity to the person or thing thus qualified. We speak of our own prayers, whether addressed to God or to His saints, as a divine service. The Psalmist speaks of us all as being gods and sons of the Most High; and yet no one takes offense, because the sense given to the words uttered is understood. Mary may be called divine because divinely chosen for the divine office of Mother" of a divine Person, Jesus Christ. (Cardinal Vaughan, preface to "True Devotion to the Blessed Virgin Mary" by St. Louis de Montfort).

and His Flesh is thy flesh; thou art united to the Lord because of thy perfect likeness to Him and by your mutual love—for thou art His Mother." And then say to her: "The Three Persons of the Godhead are with thee because thou art the Temple of the Most Blessed Trinity," and she will place you once more under the protection and care of Almighty God.

Have you become an outcast and have you been accursed by God? Then say to Our Lady: *"Blessed art thou above all women* and above all nations, by thy purity and fertility; thou hast turned God's maledictions into blessings for us," and she will bless you.

Do you hunger for the bread of grace and the bread of life? Draw near to her who bore the Living Bread Which came down from heaven, and say to her: *"Blessed be the Fruit of thy womb* Whom thou hast conceived without the slightest loss of thy virginity, Whom thou didst carry without discomfort and to Whom thou didst give birth without pain. Blessed be Jesus Who has redeemed our suffering world when we were in the bondage of sin, Who has healed the world of its sickness, Who has raised the dead to life, brought home the banished, restored sinners to a life of grace and Who has saved men from damnation." Without doubt, your soul will be filled with the bread of grace in this life and of eternal glory in the next. Amen.

Then, at the end of your prayer, pray thus with Holy Mother Church:

> *"Holy Mary*
> Holy in body and in soul
> Holy because of thy incomparable
> And eternal devotion
> To the service of God—
> Holy in thy great rank
> Of Mother of God
> Who has endowed thee
> With eminent holiness,
> A worthy attribute

Of this great dignity.
Mother of God—
And our Mother—
Our Advocate and Mediatrix
Thou who art the Treasurer of God's graces
And who dost dispense them
As thou seest fit—
Oh, we beg of thee
Obtain for us
Soon
The forgiveness of our sins—
And grant that we may be reconciled
With God's infinite Majesty.
Pray for us, sinners—
Thou who art always filled with
    compassion
For those in need—
Thou who wilt never despise sinners
Or turn them away—
For but for them
Thou wouldst never have been
Mother of the Redeemer,
Pray for us
Now,
During this short life
So fraught with sorrow and uncertainty.
Pray for us now,
Now—because we can be sure of nothing
Except the present moment.
Pray for us now
That we are being attacked night and day
By powerful and ruthless enemies . . .
Pray for us now
And at the hour of our death,
So terrible and full of danger,
When our strength is waning
And our spirits are sinking

And our souls and bodies
Are worn out with fear and pain
Pray for us then
At the hour of our death
When the devil is working
With might and main
To ensnare us and cast us into perdition.
Pray for us
At the turning point
When the die will be cast once and for all
And our lot for ever and ever
Will be heaven—
Or hell.
Come to the help of thy poor children,
Gentle Mother of pity:
And, oh, Advocate and Refuge
    of Sinners,
Protect us
At the hour of our death
And drive far from us
Our bitter enemies,
The devils our accusers,
Those with frightful presence
Fills us with dread.
Light our path
Through the valley of the shadow
    of death.
Please, Mother
Lead us
To thy Son's Judgment Seat
And do not forsake us there.
Intercede for us
And ask thy Son to forgive us
And let us into the ranks of the blessed
Thy elect
In the realm of everlasting glory.
Amen. So be it."

No one could help admiring the beauty of the Holy Rosary which is made up of two heavenly things: the Lord's Prayer and the Angelic Salutation. How could there possibly be any prayers more pleasing to Almighty God and the Blessed Virgin, or any that are easier, more precious or more helpful than these two prayers? We should always have them in our hearts and on our lips to honor the Most Blessed Trinity, Jesus Christ our Savior, and His Most Holy Mother.

In addition, at the end of each decade it is very good to add a *Gloria Patri*[2] . . . that is to say: "Glory be to the Father, and to the Son, and to the Holy Spirit. As it was in the beginning, is now, and ever shall be, world without end. Amen."

Twenty-First Rose

The Fifteen Mysteries

A MYSTERY is a sacred thing which is difficult to understand. The works of Our Lord Jesus Christ are all sacred and divine because He is God and man at one and the same time. The works of the Most Blessed Virgin are very holy because she is the most perfect and the most pure of God's creatures. The works of Our Lord and of His Blessed Mother can be rightly called mysteries because they are so full of wonders and all kinds of perfections and deep and sublime truths which the Holy Spirit reveals to the humble and simple souls who honor these mysteries.

The works of Jesus and Mary can also be called wonderful flowers; but their perfume and beauty can only be appreciated by those who study them carefully—and who

---

2. The "Gloria Patri" was a happy innovation in the recitation of the Rosary. It is quite probable that it can be attributed to Saint Louis de Montfort himself chosen for the divine office of Mother" of a divine Person, Jesus Christ (Cardinal Vaughan, preface to "True Devotion to the Blessed Virgin Mary" by St. Louis de Montfort).

open them and drink in their scent by diligent and sincere meditation.

Saint Dominic has divided up the lives of Our Lord and Our Lady into fifteen mysteries which stand for their virtues and their most important actions. These are the fifteen *tableaux* or pictures whose every detail must rule and inspire our lives. They are fifteen flaming torches to guide our steps throughout this earthly life.

They are fifteen shining mirrors which help us to know Jesus and Mary and to know ourselves as well. They will also help light the fire of their love in our hearts.

They are fifteen fiery furnaces which can consume us completely in their heavenly flames.

Our Lady taught Saint Dominic this excellent method of praying and ordered him to preach it far and wide so as to reawaken the fervor of Christians and to revive in their hearts a love for Our Blessed Lord.

She also taught it to Blessed Alan de la Roche and said to him in a vision: "When people say one hundred and fifty Angelic Salutations this prayer is very helpful to them and is a very pleasing tribute to me. But they will do better still and will please me even more if they say these salutations while meditating on the life, death and passion of Jesus Christ— for this meditation is the soul of this prayer."

For, in reality, the Rosary said without meditating on the sacred mysteries of our salvation would be almost like a body without a soul: excellent *matter* but without the *form* which is meditation—this latter being that which sets it apart from all other devotions.

The first part of the Rosary contains five mysteries: the first is the Annunciation of the Archangel Saint Gabriel to Our Lady; the second, the Visitation of Our Lady to her cousin Saint Elizabeth; the third, the Nativity of Jesus Christ; the fourth, the Presentation of the Child Jesus in the temple and the Purification of Our Lady; and the fifth, the Finding of Jesus in the Temple among the doctors.

These are called the JOYFUL MYSTERIES because of the joy

which they gave to the whole universe. Our Lady and the angels were overwhelmed with joy the moment when the Son of God was incarnate. Saint Elizabeth and Saint John the Baptist were filled with joy by the visit of Jesus and Mary. Heaven and earth rejoiced at the birth of Our Savior. Holy Simeon felt great consolation and was filled with joy when he took the Holy Child in his arms. The doctors were lost in admiration and wonderment at the answers which Jesus gave—and how could anyone describe the joy of Mary and Joseph when they found the Child Jesus after He had been lost for three days?

The second part of the Rosary is also composed of five mysteries which are called the SORROWFUL MYSTERIES because they show us Our Lord weighed down with sadness, covered with wounds, laden with insults, sufferings and torments. The first of these mysteries is Jesus' Prayer and Agony in the Garden of Olives; the second, His Scourging; the third, His Crowning with Thorns; the fourth, Jesus carrying His Cross; and the fifth, His Crucifixion and Death on Mount Calvary.

The third part of the Rosary contains five other mysteries which are called the GLORIOUS MYSTERIES because when we say them we meditate on Jesus and Mary in their triumph and glory. The first is the Resurrection of Jesus Christ; the second, His Ascension into Heaven; the third, the Descent of the Holy Ghost upon the Apostles; the fourth, Our Lady's glorious Assumption into Heaven; and the fifth, her Crowning in Heaven.

These are the fifteen fragrant flowers of the Mystical Rose Tree; devout souls fly to them like wise bees, so as to gather their nectar and make the honey of a solid devotion.

Twenty-Second Rose

Likens to Christ

THE CHIEF CONCERN of a Christian soul should be to tend to perfection. Saint Paul tells us "Be ye followers of God, as most dear children." (*Eph.* 5:1). This obligation is included in the eternal decree of our predestination, as the one and only means prescribed by God to attain everlasting glory.

Saint Gregory of Nyssa makes a delightful comparison when he says that we are all artists and that our souls are blank canvases which we have to fill in. The colors which we must use are the Christian virtues, and our Model is Jesus Christ, the perfect Living Image of God the Father. Just as a portrait painter who wants to do a good job places himself before his model and glances at him before making each stroke, so the Christian must always have the life and virtues of Jesus Christ before his eyes so that he may never say, think or do the least thing which is not in harmony with his Model.

It was because Our Lady wanted to help us in the great task of working out our salvation that she ordered Saint Dominic to teach the faithful to meditate upon the sacred mysteries of the life of Jesus Christ. She did this, not only that they might adore and glorify Him, but chiefly that they might pattern their lives and actions upon His virtues.

Children copy their parents through watching them and talking to them and they learn their own language through hearing them speak. An apprentice learns his trade through watching his master at work; in the very same way the faithful members of the Confraternity of the Holy Rosary can become like their divine Master if they reverently study and imitate the virtues of Jesus Christ which are shown in the fifteen mysteries of His life. They can do this with the help of His grace and through the intercession of His Blessed Mother.

Long ago Moses was inspired by God to command the Jewish people never to forget the graces which had been showered upon them. The Son of God, then, has all the more reason to tell us to engrave the mysteries of His life, Passion and death upon our hearts and to have them always before our eyes—because each mystery reminds us of His goodness to us in some special way and it is by these mysteries that He has shown us His overwhelming love and desire for our salvation. Our Lord is saying to us: "Oh, all of you that pass by, pause a while and see if there has ever been sorrow like unto the sorrow which I have undergone for love of you. Be mindful of My poverty and of My humiliations; think of the wine mingled with gall which I drank for you during My bitter passion."

These words and many others which could be given here should be more than enough to convince us that we must not only say the Rosary with our lips in honor of Our Lord and Our Lady, but also meditate upon the sacred mysteries while we are saying it.

Twenty-Third Rose

A Memorial

JESUS CHRIST, the divine Spouse of our souls and our very dear Friend wishes us to remember His goodness to us and all His gifts and wants us to prize them above all else. Whenever we meditate devoutly and lovingly upon the sacred mysteries of the Rosary, Our Lord has an accidental joy and so has Our Lady and all the saints in heaven.

These mysteries are the most signal results of Our Lord's love for us and the greatest presents that He could possibly give us, because it is by virtue of such presents that the Blessed Virgin Herself and all the saints are in their glory in heaven.

One day Blessed Angela of Foligno begged Our Lord to

let her know by which religious exercise she could honor Him best. He appeared to her nailed to His Cross and said: "My daughter, look at My wounds." She then realized that nothing pleases Our dear Lord more than meditation upon His sufferings. Then He showed her the wounds on His head and revealed still other sufferings to her and said: "I have suffered all this for your salvation. What can you ever do to return My love for you?"

The Holy Sacrifice of the Mass gives boundless honor to the Most Blessed Trinity because it represents the passion of Jesus Christ and because through the Mass we offer God the merits of Our Lord's obedience, of His sufferings and of His Precious Blood. The whole of the heavenly court also receives an accidental joy from the Mass. Several doctors of the Church—together with Saint Thomas Aquinas—tell us that, for the same reason, all the blessed in Heaven rejoice in the communion of the faithful because the Blessed Sacrament is a memorial of the passion and death of Jesus Christ, and that by means of it men share in its fruits and work out their salvation.

Now, the Holy Rosary, recited together with meditation on the sacred mysteries is a sacrifice of praise to God to thank Him for the great grace of our redemption. It is also a holy reminder of the sufferings, death and glory of Jesus Christ. It is therefore true that the Rosary gives glory, gives an accidental joy to Our Lord, to Our Lady and to all the blessed because they cannot desire anything greater or more contributive to our eternal happiness than to see us engaged in a practice which is so glorious for Our Lord and so salutary for ourselves.

The Gospel teaches us that a sinner who is converted and who does penance gives joy to all the angels. If the repentance and conversion of one sinner is enough to make the angels rejoice, how great must be the happiness and jubilation of the whole heavenly court and what glory for Our Blessed Lord Himself to see us here on earth meditating devoutly and lovingly on His humiliations and torments and on His cruel and ignominious death! Could anything possibly touch our hearts more surely than this and be more calculated to inspire us to true and sincere repentance?

A Christian who does not meditate on the mysteries of the Rosary is very ungrateful to Our Lord and shows how little he cares for all that our Divine Savior has suffered to save the world. This attitude seems to show that he knows little or nothing of the life of Jesus Christ, and that he has never taken the trouble to find out about Him—what He did and what He went through in order to save us.

A Christian of this kind ought to fear that having never known Jesus Christ or having put Him out of his mind and heart, He will disown him at the Day of Judgment and will say reproachfully: "Amen I say to you, I know you not." (*Matt.* 25:12). Let us, then, meditate on the life and sufferings of Our Lord by means of the Holy Rosary; let us learn to know Him well and to be grateful for all His blessings so that, at the Day of Judgment, He may number us among His children and His friends.

Twenty-Fourth Rose

Means of Perfection

THE SAINTS always made Our Lord's life the principal object of their study; they meditated on His virtues and sufferings and in this way they arrived at Christian perfection.

Once Saint Bernard began this meditation he always continued it. "At the very beginning of my conversion," he said, "I made a bouquet of myrrh made up of the sorrows of my Savior. I placed this bouquet upon my heart, thinking of the stripes, the thorns and the nails of His Passion. I used all my mental strength to meditate on these mysteries every day."

This was a practice of the Holy Martyrs too; we know how admirably they triumphed over the most cruel sufferings. Saint Bernard says that the martyrs' wonderful constancy could have only sprung from one source: their constant meditation on the wounds of Jesus Christ. The martyrs were Christ's athletes, His champions; while their blood gushed forth and their bodies were wracked with cruel torments, their generous souls were hidden in the wounds of Our Lord. These wounds made them invincible.

During her whole life the Blessed Mother's chief concern was meditation on the virtues and sufferings of her Son. When she heard the angels sing their hymns of joy at His birth and when she saw the shepherds adore Him in the stable, her heart and mind were filled with wonder and she meditated upon all these marvels. She compared the greatness of the Word Incarnate to His deep humility and the way He lowered Himself; she thought of Him in His manger filled with straw and then on His Throne in Heaven and in the bosom of His Eternal Father. She compared the might of God to the weakness of a Baby—and His wisdom to His simplicity.

One day Our Lady said to Saint Bridget: "Whenever I meditated on the beauty, modesty and wisdom of my Son, my heart was filled with joy: and whenever I thought of His hands and feet which would be pierced with cruel nails, I wept bitterly and my heart was rent with sorrow and pain."

After Our Lord's ascension Our Blessed Lady spent the rest of her life in visiting the places that had been hallowed by His presence and sufferings. When she was in those places she used to meditate upon His boundless love and upon His terrible passion.

Saint Mary Magdalene did nothing other than religious exercises of this kind during the last thirty years of her life when she lived in the prayerful seclusion of Sainte Baume.[1]

Saint Jerome says that devotion to the Holy Places was

---

1. Saint Mary Magdalene, according to a tradition, spent the last thirty years of her life in Provence, at a place subsequently called Sainte Baume ("the Holy Ointment"). Pilgrims go to the Dominican Church of Sainte Baume to venerate the relic of her head which is preserved there. (Catholic Encyclopaedia.) M.B.

widespread among the faithful in the early centuries of the Church. They came to the Holy Land from all corners of Christendom so as to impress a great love and remembrance of their Savior more deeply upon their hearts by seeing the places and things He had made holy by His birth, by His work, by His sufferings and by His death.

All Christians have but one Faith and adore one and the same God, all hoping for the same happiness in heaven. They have one Mediator Who is Jesus Christ and therefore they must all imitate their divine Model and in order to do this they must meditate on the mysteries of His life, His virtues and of His glory.

It is a great mistake to think that only priests and religious and those who have withdrawn from the turmoil of the world are supposed to meditate upon the truths of our Faith and the mysteries of the life of Jesus Christ. If priests and religious have an obligation to meditate on the great truths of our holy religion in order to live up to their vocation worthily, the same obligation, then, is just as much incumbent upon the laity—because of the fact that every day they meet with spiritual dangers which might make them lose their souls. Therefore they should arm themselves with the frequent meditation on the life, virtues and sufferings of Our Blessed Lord—which are so beautifully contained in the fifteen mysteries of the Holy Rosary.

Twenty-Fifth Rose

Wealth of Sanctification

NEVER WILL ANYONE really be able to understand the marvelous riches of sanctification which are contained in the prayers and mysteries of the Holy Rosary. This meditation on the mysteries of the life and death of Our Lord and Savior Jesus Christ is the source of the most wonderful fruits for those who use it.

Today people want things that strike and move and that leave deep impressions on the soul. Nor has there ever been anything in the whole history of the world more moving than the wonderful story of the life, death and glory of Our Savior which is contained in the Holy Rosary. In the fifteen tableaux the chief scenes or mysteries of His life unfold before our eyes. How could there ever be any prayers more wonderful and sublime than the Lord's Prayer and the Salutation of the Angel? All our desires and all our needs are found expressed in these two prayers.

The meditation on the mysteries and the prayers of the Rosary is the easiest of all prayers, because the diversity of the virtues of Our Lord Jesus Christ and the different stages of His life which we study refresh and fortify our mind in a wonderful way and help us to avoid distractions.

For learned people these mysteries are the source of the most profound doctrine but simple people find in them a means of instruction well within their reach.

We must learn this easy form of meditation before progressing to the highest state of contemplation. This is the view of Saint Thomas Aquinas and the advice that he gives when he says that first of all one must practice on a battlefield, as it were, by acquiring all the virtues which the Holy Rosary gives us to imitate. The learned Cajetan says that this is the way that we reach a really intimate union with God—for without this union contemplation is nothing other than a dangerous illusion which can lead souls astray.

If only the Illuminists or the Quietists[1] of today had followed this piece of advice they would never have fallen so low nor would they have caused such scandals and upset the devotions of good people. To think that it is possible to say prayers that are finer and more beautiful than the Our Father and the Hail Mary is to fall prey to a strange illusion of the devil.

---

1. Quietism and Illuminism were heresies of Saint Louis' day. Adherents of the former school and also those of the latter had an exaggerated idea of divine inspiration and denied the necessity of individual effort in the spiritual life. Madame Guillon was the chief exponent of Quietism in France. M.B.

These heavenly prayers are the support, the strength and the safeguard of our souls—but I must admit that it is not always necessary to say them as vocal prayers. It is quite true that, in a sense, mental prayer is more perfect than vocal prayer, but, believe me, it is really dangerous not to say fatal to give up saying the Rosary of your own accord under the excuse of seeking a more perfect union with God.

Sometimes a soul that is proud in a subtle way and who may have done everything that he can do interiorly to rise to the sublime heights of contemplation that the Saints have reached, may be deluded by the noon-day devil into giving up his former devotions because he thinks that he has found a greater good. He then looks upon his erstwhile practices as inferior and only fit for ordinary and mediocre souls.

But this kind of soul has deliberately turned a deaf ear to the prayers and salutation taught us by an archangel and even to the Prayer which God made and taught us and which He said Himself. "Thus therefore shall you pray: Our Father . . ." (*Matt.* 6:9). Having reached this point such a soul drifts from its first illusion into still greater ones and falls from precipice to precipice.

Believe me, dear brothers of the Rosary Confraternity, if you genuinely wish to reach a high level of prayer in all honesty and without falling into the traps that the devil sets for those who pray, say your whole Rosary every day, or at least five decades of it.

If, by the grace of God, you have already reached a high level of prayer, keep up the practice of saying the Holy Rosary if you wish to remain in that state and if you hope, through it, to grow in humility. For never will anyone who says his Rosary every day become a formal heretic or be led astray by the devil. This is a statement that I would gladly sign with my blood.

On the other hand if Almighty God in His infinite mercy draws you to Him as forcibly as He did some of the Saints while saying the Rosary, make yourself passive in His hands and let yourself be drawn towards Him. Let God work and pray in you and let Him say your Rosary in His way and this will be enough for the day.

But if you are still in the state of active contemplation or the usual prayer of quietude, which is to say that of placing yourself in the presence of God and loving Him, you have every reason in the world not to give up saying your Rosary. Far from making you lose ground in mental prayer or stunting your spiritual growth, it will be the most tremendous help to you. You will find that it will be a real Jacob's ladder with fifteen rungs and by each one of these you will go from virtue to virtue and from light to light. Thus, without danger of being misled, you will easily come to the fullness of the age of Jesus Christ.

Twenty-Sixth Rose

Sublime Prayer

WHATEVER YOU DO, do not be like a certain pious but self-willed lady in Rome, so often referred to when speaking about the Rosary. She was so devout and so fervent that she put to shame by her holy life, even the strictest religious in the Church.

Having decided to ask Saint Dominic's advice about her spiritual life she asked him to hear her confession. For penance he gave her one whole Rosary to say and advised her to say it every day. She said that she had no time to say it, excusing herself on the grounds that she made the Stations[1] of Rome every day, that she wore sack-cloth and also a hair shirt, that she gave herself the discipline several times a week, that she carried out so many other penances and fasted so much. Saint Dominic urged her over and over again to take his advice and say the Rosary, but she would

---

1. This is a devotion that originated in the very early Church; it consists in visiting certain stational churches in Rome and saying prescribed prayers in each one. This practice was usually penitential. (Catholic Encyclopedia). M.B.

not hear of it. She left the confessional, horrified at the tactics of this new spiritual director who had tried so hard to persuade her to take on a devotion that was not at all to her liking.

Later on when she was in prayer she fell into ecstasy and had a vision of her soul appearing before Our Lord's Judgment Seat. Saint Michael put all her penances and other prayers onto one balance of the scales and all her sins and imperfections onto the other. The tray of her good works was greatly outweighed by that of her sins and imperfections.

Filled with terror she cried for mercy, imploring the help of the Blessed Virgin, her gracious Advocate, who took the one and only Rosary that she had said for her penance and dropped it onto the tray of her good works. This one Rosary was so heavy that it weighed more than all her sins as well as all her good works. Our Lady then reproved her for having refused to follow the counsel of her servant Dominic and for not saying the Rosary every day.

As soon as she came to herself she rushed and threw herself at the feet of Saint Dominic and told him all that had happened, begged his forgiveness for her unbelief and promised to say the Rosary faithfully every day. By this means she rose to Christian perfection and finally to the glory of everlasting life.

You who are people of prayer—learn from this how tremendous is the power, the value and the importance of this devotion of the Most Holy Rosary when it is said together with meditation on the mysteries.

Few saints have reached the same heights of prayer as Saint Mary Magdalene who was lifted up to Heaven each day by angels, and who had had the privilege of learning at the feet of Our Lord Himself and His Blessed Mother. Yet one day when she asked God to show her a sure way of advancing in His love and of arriving at the height of perfection, He sent Saint Michael the Archangel to tell her, on His behalf, that there was no other way for her to arrive at perfection than to meditate on Our Lord's passion. So he placed a cross in the front of her cave and told her to pray before it, contemplating the Sorrowful Mysteries which she had seen take place with her own eyes.

The example of Saint Francis de Sales, the great spiritual director of his time, should spur you on to join the holy confraternity of the Rosary, since, great saint that he was, he bound himself by oath to say the whole Rosary every single day as long as he lived.

Saint Charles Borromeo said it every day also and strongly recommended the devotion to his priests and to the ecclesiastics in the seminaries and also to all his people.

Saint Pius V, one of the greatest Popes who have ever ruled the Church, said the Rosary every day. Saint Thomas of Villanova, Archbishop of Valence, Saint Ignatius, Saint Francis Xavier, Saint Francis Borgia, Saint Theresa and Saint Philip Neri as well as many other great men whom I have not mentioned were deeply devoted to the Holy Rosary.

Follow their example; your spiritual directors will be pleased and if they are aware of the benefit that you can derive from this devotion, they will be the very first to urge you to adopt it.

Twenty-Seventh Rose

Benefits

I SHOULD LIKE to give you even more reason for embracing this devotion which so many great souls have practiced; the Rosary recited with meditation on the mysteries brings about the following marvelous results:
1. it gradually gives us a perfect knowledge of Jesus Christ;
2. it purifies our souls, washing away sin;
3. it gives us victory over all our enemies;
4. it makes it easy for us to practice virtue;
5. it sets us on fire with love of Our Blessed Lord;
6. it enriches us with graces and merits;

7. it supplies us with what is needed to pay all our debts to God and to our fellow men, and finally, it obtains all kinds of graces for us from Almighty God.

The knowledge of Jesus Christ is the science of Christians and the science of salvation; Saint Paul says that it surpasses all human sciences in value and perfection." (Cf. *Phil.* 3:8). This is true:

1. because of the dignity of its object, which is a God-man compared to Whom the whole universe is but a drop of dew or a grain of sand;

2. because of its helpfulness to us; human sciences, on the other hand, but fill us with the smoke and emptiness of pride;

3. and finally, because of its utter necessity: for no one can possibly be saved without the knowledge of Jesus Christ— and yet a man who knows absolutely nothing of any of the other sciences will be saved as long as he is illumined by the science of Jesus Christ.

Blessed is the Rosary which gives us this science and knowledge of our Blessed Lord through our meditations on His life, death, passion and glory.

The Queen of Saba, lost in admiration at Solomon's wisdom cried out: "Blessed are thy men and blessed are thy servants who stand before thee always, and hear thy wisdom." (*3 Kgs.* 10:8). But far happier still are the faithful who carefully meditate on the life, virtues, suffering and glory of Our Savior, because by this means they can gain the perfect knowledge in which eternal life consists. "This is eternal life." (*John* 17:3).

Our Lady revealed to Blessed Alan that no sooner had Saint Dominic begun preaching the Rosary than hardened sinners were touched and wept bitterly over their grievous sins. Young children performed incredible penances and everywhere that he preached the Holy Rosary such fervor arose that sinners changed their lives and edified everyone by their penances and change of heart.

If by chance your conscience is burdened with sin, take

your Rosary and say at least part of it, honoring some of the mysteries of the life, passion or glory of Our Lord Jesus Christ, and be sure that, while you are meditating upon these mysteries and honoring them He will show His sacred wounds to His Father in Heaven. He will plead for you and will obtain for you contrition and the forgiveness of your sins.

One day Our Lord said to Blessed Alan: "If only these poor wretched sinners would say My Rosary, they would share in the merits of My passion and I would be their Advocate and would appease My Father's Justice."

This life is nothing but warfare and a series of temptations; we do not have to contend with enemies of flesh and blood but with the very powers of Hell. What better weapons could we possibly use to combat them than the Prayer which our great Captain taught us, and the Angelic Salutation which has chased away devils, destroyed sin and renewed the world? What better weapon could we use than meditation on the life and passion of Our Lord and Savior Jesus Christ? For, as Saint Peter says, it is with this thought we must arm ourselves in order to defend ourselves against the very same enemies which he conquered and which molest us every day. (Cf. *1 Ptr.* 4:1).

"Ever since the devil was crushed by the humility and passion of Jesus Christ he has been very nearly unable to attack a soul that is armed with meditation on the mysteries of Our Lord's life, and, if he does trouble such a soul, he is sure to be shamefully defeated." (Cardinal Hugues.)

"Put you on the armor of God." (*Eph.* 6:11). So arm yourselves with the arms of God—with the Holy Rosary—and you will crush the devil's head and you will stand firm in the face of all his temptations. This is why even the material rosary itself is such a terrible thing for the devil, and why the saints have used it to enchain devils and to chase them out of the bodies of people who were possessed. Such happenings are reported in more than one authentic record.

Blessed Alan said that a man he knew of had desperately

tried all kinds of devotions to rid himself of the evil spirit who possessed him, but without success. Finally he thought of wearing his Rosary around his neck, which eased him considerably. He discovered that whenever he took it off the devil tormented him cruelly, so he resolved to wear it night and day. This drove the evil spirit away forever, because he could not bear such a terrible chain. Blessed Alan also testified that he had delivered a large number of people who were possessed by putting the Rosary around their necks.

Father Jean Amat, of the Order of St. Dominic, was giving a series of Lenten sermons in the Kingdom of Aragon one year, when a young girl was brought to him who was possessed by the devil. After he had exorcised her several times without success he put his rosary around her neck. Hardly had he done so than the girl began to scream and yell in a fearful way, shrieking: "Take them off! Take them off! These beads are torturing me!" At last the Father, filled with pity for the girl, took his rosary off her.

The very next night when Father Amat was in bed, the same devils who had possession of the girl came to him foaming with rage and tried to seize him. But he had his rosary clasped in his hand and no efforts of theirs could wrench it from him. He managed to beat them with it very well indeed and chased them away, crying out: "Holy Mary, Our Lady of the Holy Rosary, come to my help!"

The next day when he went to the Church he met the poor girl—still possessed—and one of the devils within her started to laugh and said in a mocking voice: "Well, Brother, if you had been without your rosary, we should have made short shrift of you!" Then the good Father threw his rosary around the girl's neck without more ado and said: "By the sacred name of Jesus and that of Mary His Holy Mother, and by the power of the Most Holy Rosary I command you, evil spirits, to leave the body of this girl," and they were immediately forced to obey and she was delivered from them.

These stories show the power of the Holy Rosary in overcoming all possible temptations that evil spirits may bring—and also all kinds of sin—because these blessed beads put devils to rout.

Twenty-Eighth Rose

Salutary Effects

SAINT AUGUSTINE says quite emphatically that there is no spiritual exercise more fruitful or more useful to our salvation than continually turning our thoughts to the sufferings of Our Savior.

Blessed Albert the Great who had Saint Thomas Aquinas as his disciple learned in a revelation that by simply thinking of or meditating on the passion of Our Lord Jesus Christ, a Christian gains more merit than if he had fasted on bread and water every Friday for a whole year, or had beaten himself with his discipline once a week until the blood flowed, or had recited the whole Book of Psalms every day. If this is so, then how great must be the merit that we can gain by the Holy Rosary which commemorates the whole life and passion of Our Savior!

One day Our Lady revealed to Blessed Alan that, after the Holy Sacrifice of the Mass, which is the most important as well as the living memorial of Our Blessed Lord's passion there could not possibly be a finer devotion or one of greater merit than that of the Holy Rosary, which is like a second memorial and representation of the life and passion of Our Lord Jesus Christ.

Father Dorland says that in 1481 Our Lady appeared to Venerable Dominic, the Carthusian, who lived at Treves, and said to him: "Whenever one of the faithful who is in a state of grace says the Rosary while meditating on the mysteries of the life and passion of Jesus Christ, he obtains full and entire remission of all his sins."

Our Lady also said to Blessed Alan: "I want you to know

that, although there are numerous indulgences already attached to the recitation of my Rosary, I shall add many more to every fifty Hail Marys (each group of five decades) for those who say them devoutly, on their knees—being, of course, free from mortal sin. And whosoever shall persevere in the devotion of the Holy Rosary, saying these prayers and meditations, shall be rewarded for it; I shall obtain for him full remission of the penalty and of the guilt of all his sins at the end of his life. Do not be unbelieving, as though this is impossible. It is easy for me to do because I am the Mother of the King of heaven, and He calls me full of grace. And, being full of grace, I am able to dispense grace freely to my dear children."

Saint Dominic was so convinced of the efficacy of the Holy Rosary and of its great value that, when he heard confessions, he hardly ever gave any other penance. You have seen an example of this already in the story that I told you of the lady in Rome to whom he gave one single Rosary for her penance. Saint Dominic was a great saint and other confessors should be sure to walk in his footsteps by asking their penitents to say the Rosary together with meditation on the sacred mysteries, rather than giving them other penances which are less meritorious and less pleasing to God, less likely to help them advance in virtue and not as efficacious as the Rosary for helping them avoid falling into sin. Moreover, while saying the Rosary, people gain countless indulgences which are not attached to many other devotions.

And, as Abbe Blosius says: "The Rosary, with meditation on the life and passion of Jesus Christ, is certainly most pleasing to Our Lord and His Blessed Mother and is a very successful means of obtaining all graces; we can say it for ourselves as well as for others for whom we wish to pray and for the whole Church. Let us turn, then, to the Holy Rosary in all our needs, and we shall infallibly obtain the graces we ask of God to save our souls."

Twenty-Ninth Rose

Means of Salvation

SAINT DENIS said that there is nothing more noble and more pleasing to God than to cooperate in the work of saving souls and to frustrate the devil's plans for ruining them. The Son of God came down to earth for no other reason than to save souls.

He upset Satan's empire by founding the Church, but the former rallied his strength and wreaked cruel violence on souls by the Albigensian heresy, by the hatred, dissensions and abominable vices which he spread throughout the world in the XIth, XIIth and XIIIth centuries.

Only stringent measures could possibly cure such terrible disorders and repel Satan's forces. The Blessed Virgin, Protectress of the Church, has given us a most powerful means for appeasing her Son's anger, uprooting heresy and reforming Christian morals, in the Confraternity of the Holy Rosary. It has proved its worth for it has brought back charity and frequent reception of the Sacraments which flourished in the first golden centuries of the Church and it has reformed Christian morals.

Pope Leo X said in his Bull that this Confraternity had been founded in honor of God and of the Blessed Virgin as a wall to hold back the evils that were going to break upon the Church.

Gregory XIII said that the Rosary was given us from Heaven as a means of appeasing God's anger and of imploring Our Lady's intercession.

Jules III said that the Rosary was inspired by God in order that Heaven might be more easily opened to us through the favors of Our Lady.

Paul III and Saint Pius V stated that the Rosary was given to the faithful in order that they might have spiritual peace and consolation more easily. Surely everyone will want to join a confraternity which was founded for such noble purposes.

Father Dominic, the Carthusian, who was deeply devoted to the Holy Rosary, had this vision: Heaven was opened for him to see and the whole heavenly court was assembled in magnificent array. He heard them sing the Rosary in an enchanting melody and each decade was in honor of a mystery of the life, passion or glory of our Lord Jesus Christ and of His Blessed Mother. Father Dominic noticed that whenever they said the sacred name of Mary they bowed their heads and at the name of Jesus they genuflected and gave thanks to God for the great good that He had wrought in Heaven and on earth through the Holy Rosary, which the Confraternity members say here on earth. He noticed too that they were praying for those who practice this devotion. He also saw beautiful crowns without number which were made of gorgeous perfumed flowers held in readiness for those who say the Holy Rosary devoutly. He learned that by every Rosary that they say they make a crown for themselves which they will be able to wear in Heaven.

This holy Carthusian's vision is very much like that which Saint John the Beloved Disciple had. He had a vision of a very great multitude of angels and saints who continually praised and blessed Our Savior Jesus Christ for all that He had done and suffered on earth for our salvation. This is precisely what the devout members of the Rosary Confraternity do.

It must not be thought that the Rosary is only for women and for simple and ignorant people; it is also for men and for the greatest of men. As soon as Saint Dominic acquainted Pope Innocent III with the fact that he had received a command from Heaven to establish the Confraternity of the Most Holy Rosary, the Holy Father gave it his full approval, urged Saint Dominic to preach it and said that he wished to become a member himself. Many Cardinals embraced the devotion with great fervor too, which prompted Lopez to say: "Neither sex nor age nor any other condition has kept anyone from devotion to the Holy Rosary."

Members of the Confraternity have always been from all

walks of life: dukes, princes, kings, as well as prelates, cardinals and Sovereign Pontiffs; it would take too long to give all their names in this little book, which is but a summary. If you join the Confraternity, dear reader, you will share in the devotion of your fellow members and in the graces that they gain on earth as well as in their glory in heaven. "Since you are united to them in their devotion you will share in their dignity."

Thirtieth Rose

Confraternity Privileges[1]

IF THE VALUE of a confraternity and the advisability of joining it are to be judged by the indulgences attached to it, then it can surely be said that the Confraternity of the Most Holy Rosary is by far the most valuable one and that the faithful should be strongly urged to join it. This is because it has been awarded more indulgences than any other confraternity in the Church, and ever since its inception there has hardly been a Pope who has not opened up the Treasures of the Church to enrich it with further privileges.

Knowing that a good example is more compelling than glowing words and even favors, Sovereign Pontiffs have found that there was no better way to show their high regard for the confraternity than to join it themselves.

Here is a short summary of the indulgences which they wholeheartedly granted to the Confraternity of the Holy Rosary and which were confirmed again by our Holy Father Pope Innocent XI on July 31, 1679 and received and made public on September 25th of the same year by His Excellency the Archbishop of Paris:

1. Members may gain a plenary indulgence on the day of

---

1. Leo XIII modified this list of indulgences. We give it here because it is included in Saint Louis' manuscript.

joining the confraternity;

2. A plenary indulgence at the hour of death;

3. For each three groups of Five Mysteries recited: ten years and ten quarantines;

4. Each time that members say the holy names of Jesus and Mary devoutly: seven days' indulgences;

5. Seven years and seven quarantines may be gained by those who devoutly take part in or attend the Holy Rosary Procession;

6. Members who have made a good confession and who are genuinely sorry for their sins may gain a plenary indulgence on certain days by visiting the Holy Rosary Chapel in the Church where the Confraternity is established. This plenary indulgence can be gained on the First Sunday of every month, and on the feasts of Our Lord and Our Lady.

7. For assisting at the Salve Regina[2] one hundred days' indulgence;

8. Those who openly wear the Holy Rosary out of devotion and to set a good example may gain one hundred days' indulgence;

9. Sick members who are not able to go to Church may gain a plenary indulgence by going to confession and receiving Holy Communion and by saying that day the whole Rosary if possible, or at least five decades;

10. Our Sovereign Pontiffs have shown their generosity towards members of the Rosary Confraternity by allowing them to gain the indulgences attached to the Stations of Rome by visiting five altars in the Church where the Rosary Confraternity is established, and by saying the Our Father and Hail Mary five times before each altar, for the happy estate of the Church. If there are only one or two altars in the Confraternity Church they should

---

2. The Salve Regina is sung in procession after Compline by the Fathers and Brothers in every Dominican monastery, and also by Dominican Sisters. This custom was started by St. Dominic . . . Since then other orders and congregations have adopted this practice. M. B.

recite the Our Father and Hail Mary twenty-five times before one of them.

This is a wonderful favor granted to Confraternity members for in the Stational Churches in Rome plenary indulgences can be gained, souls can be delivered from Purgatory and many other great indulgences too can be gained by members with very little effort and no expense and without leaving their own country. And even if the Confraternity is not established in the place where the members live they can gain the very same indulgences by visiting five altars in any Church. This concession was granted by Leo X.

The Sacred Congregation of Indulgences drew up a list of certain definite days upon which those outside the city of Rome could gain the Indulgences of the Stations of Rome. The Holy Father approved this list on March 7th, 1678, and commanded that it be strictly observed. These indulgences can be gained on the following days:

All the Sundays of Advent; each of the three Ember Days; also Christmas Eve, at Midnight Mass, the Daybreak Mass and at the Third Mass; the feast of Saint Stephen; that of Saint John the Evangelist; the feast of the Holy Innocents; the Circumcision and the Epiphany; the Sundays of Septuagesima, Sexagesima, Quinquagesima and on every single day from Ash Wednesday to Low Sunday inclusively; each of the three Rogation Days; Ascension Day; the Vigil of Pentecost; every day during the octave; and on each of the three September Ember Days.

Dear Confraternity members, there are numerous other indulgences which you can gain. If you want to know about them look up the complete list of indulgences which have been granted to members of the Rosary Confraternity. You will see the names of the Popes in question, the years in which they granted the indulgences and many other particulars which I have not been able to include in this little summary.

Thirty-First Rose

Blanche of Castille—Alphonsus VIII

BLANCHE OF CASTILLE, Queen of France, was deeply grieved because twelve years after her marriage she was still childless. When Saint Dominic went to see her he advised her to say her Rosary every day to ask God for the grace of motherhood, and she faithfully carried out his advice. In 1213 she gave birth to her eldest child, Philip, but the child died in infancy.

The Queen's fervor was nowise dulled by this disappointment; on the contrary, she sought Our Lady's help more than ever before. She had a large number of Rosaries given out to all members of the court and also to people in several cities of the Kingdom, asking them to join her in entreating God for a blessing that this time would be complete. Thus, in 1215, Saint Louis was born—the prince who was to become the glory of France and the model of all Christian kings.

Alphonsus VIII, King of Aragon and Castille, had been leading a disorderly life and therefore had been punished by God in several ways, one of these being that he was worsted in battle and had to take refuge in a city belonging to one of his allies.

Saint Dominic happened to be in this city on Christmas Day and preached on the Holy Rosary as he always did, pointing out how great are the graces that we can obtain through it. He mentioned, among other things, that those who said the Rosary devoutly would overcome their enemies and would regain all that they had lost in warfare.

The King listened attentively and sent for Saint Dominic to ask if what he had said about the Rosary was really true. Saint Dominic assured him that nothing was more true, and that if only he would practice this devotion and join the Confraternity, he would see for himself. The King firmly resolved to say his Rosary every day and perservered for a year in doing so. The very next Christmas Our Lady appeared to him at the end of his Rosary and said: "Alphonsus, you have served me for a year by saying my Rosary devoutly every day, so I have come to reward you: I have obtained the forgiveness of your sins from my Son. And I am going to give you this rosary; wear it, and I promise you that none of your enemies will ever be able to harm you again."

Our Lady vanished leaving the King overjoyed and greatly encouraged; he immediately went in search of the Queen to tell her all about Our Lady's gift and the promise that went with it. He held the rosary to her eyes (she had been blind for some time) and her sight was instantly restored.

Shortly afterwards the King rallied some troops with the help of his allies and boldly attacked his enemies. He forced them to give back the territory that they had taken from him and to make amends for their other offences against him, and put them completely to rout. In fact, he became so lucky in war that soldiers rushed from all sides to fight under his standard because it seemed that whenever he went to battle the victory was sure to be his.

This is not surprising because he never went to battle without first saying his Rosary devoutly on his knees. He made certain that all the members of his court joined the Confraternity of the Most Holy Rosary and he also saw that his officers and servants were devoted to it.

The Queen joined the Confraternity and started saying the Rosary too, and she and her husband persevered in Our Lady's service and lived really holy lives.

Thirty-Second Rose

Don Perez

SAINT DOMINIC had a cousin named Don Perez, or Pedro, who was leading a highly immoral life. When he heard that his cousin was preaching on the wonders of the Rosary and learned that several people had been converted and had amended their lives by means of it, he said:

"I had given up all hope of being saved but now I am beginning to take heart again. I really must hear this man of God." So one day he went to hear one of Saint Dominic's sermons. When the latter caught sight of him he struck out against sin more zealously than ever before, and from the depths of his heart he besought Almighty God to enlighten his cousin and to let him see what a deplorable state his soul was in.

At first Don Perez was somewhat alarmed, but he still did not resolve to change his ways. He came once more to hear Saint Dominic preach and his cousin, realizing that a heart as hard as his could only be moved by something quite out of the ordinary, cried out with a loud voice: "Oh Lord Jesus, grant that this whole congregation may actually see the state of the man who has just come into Your House."

Then everybody suddenly saw that Don Perez was completely surrounded by a band of devils in the form of hideous beasts who were holding him in great iron chains. People fled hither and thither in abject terror and Don Perez himself was even more appalled than they when he saw how everyone shunned him.

Saint Dominic told them all to stand still and said to his cousin: "Unhappy man that you are, acknowledge the deplorable state you are in and throw yourself at Our Lady's feet. Take this Rosary; say it with devotion and with true sorrow for all your sins, and make a firm resolution to amend your life."

So Don Perez knelt down and said the whole Rosary; he then felt the need of making his confession and did so with heartfelt contrition. Saint Dominic ordered him to say the Rosary every day; he promised to do so and he entered his name on the Rosary Confraternity list in his own hand.

When he left the Church his face was no longer horrible to behold but had a glow like that of an angel's. Thereafter he persevered in devotion to the Holy Rosary, led a well-ordered Christian life and died a happy death.

Thirty-Third Rose

A Diabolical Possession

WHEN SAINT DOMINIC was preaching the Rosary near Carcassone[1] an Albigensian was brought to him who was possessed by the devil. Saint Dominic exorcised him in the presence of a great crowd of people; it appears that over twelve thousand had come to hear him preach. The devils who were in possession of this wretched man were forced to answer Saint Dominic's questions in spite of themselves. They said that:

1. There were fifteen thousand of them in the body of this poor man, because he had attacked the fifteen mysteries of the Rosary;
2. They went on to testify that by preaching the Rosary he put fear and horror into the very depths of hell and that he was the man they hated most throughout the whole world, because of the souls which he snatched from them through devotion to the Holy Rosary;
3. They then revealed several other things.

Saint Dominic put his rosary around the Albigensian's neck and asked the devils to tell him who, of all the saints in heaven, was the one they feared the most, and who should therefore be the most loved and revered by men. At this they let out such unearthly screams that most of the people fell to the ground, faint from fear. Then, using all their cunning, so as not to answer, the devils wept and wailed in such a pitiful way that many of the people wept also, out of purely natural pity. The devils spoke through the mouth of the Albigensian, pleading in a heartrending voice:

"Dominic, Dominic, have mercy on us—we promise you

---

1. This incident is referred to by Saint Louis in his "True Devotion to the Blessed Virgin Mary" when he explains that those who love Our Lady are not lost. Cf. paragraph 42. M.B.

that we will never hurt you. You have always had compassion for sinners and those in distress; have pity on us, for we are in grievous straits. We are suffering so very much already, so why do you delight in heightening our pains? Can't you be satisfied with our suffering without adding to it? Have pity on us! Have pity on us!"

Saint Dominic was not one whit moved by the pathos of these wretched spirits and told them that he would not let them alone until they had answered his question. Then they said they would whisper the answer in such a way that only Saint Dominic would be able to hear. The latter firmly insisted upon their answering clearly and out loud. Then the devils kept quiet and refused to say another word, completely disregarding Saint Dominic's orders—so he knelt down and prayed thus to Our Lady: "Oh, all powerful and wonderful Virgin Mary, I implore you by the power of the Most Holy Rosary, order these enemies of the human race to answer me."

No sooner had he made this prayer than a glowing flame leaped out of the ears, nostrils and mouth of the Albigensian. Everyone shook with fear, but the fire did not hurt anyone. Then the devils cried:

"Dominic, we beseech you, by the passion of Jesus Christ and by the merits of His Holy Mother and of all the saints, let us leave the body of this man without speaking further— for the angels will answer your question whenever you wish. After all, are we not liars? So why should you want to believe us? Please don't torture us any more; have pity on us."

"Woe unto you wretched spirits, who do not deserve to be heard," Saint Dominic said, and kneeling down he prayed to Our Lady:

"Oh most worthy Mother of Wisdom, I am praying for the people assembled here who have already learned how to say the Angelic Salutation properly. Please, I beg of you, force your enemies to proclaim the whole truth and nothing but the truth about this, here and now, before the multitude."

Saint Dominic had hardly finished this prayer when he saw the Blessed Virgin near at hand, surrounded by a multitude of angels. She struck the possessed man with a golden rod that she held and said: "Answer my servant Dominic at once." (Remember, the people neither saw nor heard Our Lady, but only Saint Dominic.) Then the devils started screaming:

"Oh you who are our enemy, our downfall and our destruction, why have you come from heaven just to torture us so grievously? O Advocate of sinners, you who snatch them from the very jaws of hell, you who are the very sure path to heaven, must we, in spite of ourselves, tell the whole truth and confess before everyone who it is who is the cause of our shame and our ruin? Oh woe unto us, princes of darkness:

"Then listen well, you Christians: the Mother of Jesus Christ is all-powerful and she can save her servants from falling into hell. She is the Sun which destroys the darkness of our wiles and subtlety. It is she who uncovers our hidden plots, breaks our snares and makes our temptations useless and ineffectual.

"We have to say, however reluctantly, that not a single soul who has really persevered in her service has ever been damned with us; one single sigh that she offers to the Blessed Trinity is worth far more than all the prayers, desires and aspirations of all the saints.

"We fear her more than all the other saints in heaven together and we have no success with her faithful servants. Many Christians who call upon her when they are at the hour of death and who really ought to be damned according to our ordinary standards are saved by her intercession.

"Oh if only that Mary (it is thus in their fury that they called her) had not pitted her strength against ours and had not upset our plans, we should have conquered the Church and should have destroyed it long before this; and we would have seen to it that all the Orders in the Church fell into error and disorder.

"Now that we are forced to speak we must also tell you this: nobody who perseveres in saying the Rosary will be damned, because she obtains for her servants the grace of true contrition for their sins and by means of this they obtain God's forgiveness and mercy."

Then Saint Dominic had them all say the Rosary very slowly and with great devotion, and a wonderful thing happened: at each Hail Mary that he and the people said together a large group of devils issued forth from the wretched man's body under the guise of red-hot coals.

When the devils had all been expelled and the heretic was at last entirely free of them, Our Lady (who was still invisible) gave her blessing to the assembled company, and they were filled with joy because of this.

A large number of heretics were converted because of this miracle and joined the Confraternity of the Most Holy Rosary.

Thirty-Fourth Rose

Simon de Montfort, Alan de Lanvallay and Othère

IT IS ALMOST impossible to do real credit to the victories that Count Simon de Montfort won against the Albigensians under the patronage of Our Lady of the Rosary. These victories are so famous that the world has never seen anything to match them. One day he defeated ten thousand heretics with a force of five hundred men and on another occasion he overcame three thousand with only thirty men. Finally, with eight hundred horsemen and one thousand infantrymen he completely put to rout the army of the King of Aragon which was a hundred thousand strong, and this with the loss on his side of only one horseman and eight soldiers!

Our Lady also protected Alan de Lanvallay, a Breton

Knight, from great perils. He too was fighting for the Faith against the Albigensians. One day when he found himself surrounded by enemies on all sides Our Lady let fall one hundred and fifty rocks upon his enemies and he was delivered from their hands. Another day when his ship foundered and was about to sink, the Blessed Mother caused one hundred and fifty small hills to appear miraculously above the water and by means of them they reached Brittany in safety.

He built a monastery at Dinan for the religious of St. Dominic, in thanksgiving to Our Lady for all the miracles that she had worked on his behalf in answer to his daily Rosary. Having become a religious himself he died a holy death at Orleans.

Othère was also a Breton soldier, from Vaucouleurs, and he often put whole companies of heretics or robbers to flight unaided, wearing his Rosary on his arm or carrying it on the hilt of his sword. Once when he had beaten them his enemies admitted that they had seen his sword gleam and that another time they had noticed a shield on his arm which had pictures of Our Lord and Our Lady and the saints upon it. This shield made him invisible and gave him the strength to attack well.

Another time he defeated twenty thousand heretics with only ten companies and without losing a single man. This so impressed the general of the heretics' army that he came to see Othère afterwards, abjured his heresy and declared publicly that he had seen him surrounded by flaming swords during the battle.

Thirty-Fifth Rose

Cardinal Pierre

BLESSED ALAN says that a certain Cardinal Pierre, whose titular Church was that of St. Mary-beyond-the-Tiber, was a great friend of Saint Dominic's and had learned from him a deep devotion to the Most Holy Rosary. This resulted in his loving it so much that he never ceased singing its praises and encouraging everyone he met to embrace it.

Eventually he was sent as Legate to the Holy Land to the Christians who were fighting the Saracens. So successfully did he convince the Christian army of the power of the Rosary that they started saying it one and all to storm heaven for help in a battle in which they knew they would be pitifully outnumbered. This resulted in victory for them, and three thousand Christians triumphed over an enemy of one hundred thousand.

As we have seen, the devils have an overwhelming fear of the Rosary. Saint Bernard says that the Angelic Salutation puts them to flight and makes all Hell tremble.

Blessed Alan says that he has seen several people delivered from Satan's bondage after taking up the Holy Rosary, even though they had previously sold themselves to him in body and soul by renouncing their Baptismal Vows and their allegiance to Our Lord Jesus Christ.

Thirty-Sixth Rose

Freed from Satan

IN 1578 A WOMAN in Anvers had given herself to the devil and had signed the contract with her own blood. Shortly afterwards she was stricken with sincere remorse and had an intense desire to make amends for this terrible deed. So she sought out a kind and wise confessor who advised her to go to Father Henry, one of the Fathers of the Dominican Friary, who was Director of the Rosary Confraternity in that town, to ask him to enroll her in it and hear her confession.

Accordingly she went to ask for him but met, not Father Henry, but the devil disguised as a Dominican Father. The latter scolded her pitilessly and said that she could never hope to receive Almighty God's grace again as long as she lived, and that there was absolutely no way in which she could regain possession of her contract. This grieved her greatly but she did not quite lose hope of God's mercy and sought out Father Henry once more, only to find the devil a second time, and to meet with a second rebuff. She came back for the third time and then at last, by Divine Providence, she found Father Henry in person—the priest whom she had been looking for—and he treated her with very great kindness, urging her to throw herself upon the mercy of Almighty God and to make a good confession. He then received her into the Confraternity and told her to say the Rosary frequently.

One day while Father Henry was saying Mass for her Our Lady forced the devil to give her back the contract which she had signed. In this way she was delivered from the devil by the authority of Mary and by her devotion to the Most Holy Rosary.

Thirty-Seventh Rose

A Monastery Reformed

A NOBLEMAN who had several daughters entered one of them in a lax monastery where the nuns were very proud and thought of nothing else but worldly pleasures. The nuns' confessor, on the other hand, was a zealous priest and had a great love for the Holy Rosary. Wishing to guide this nun into a better way of life he ordered her to say the Rosary every day in honor of the Blessed Virgin while meditating on the life, passion and glory of Jesus Christ.

She joyously undertook to say the Rosary and little by little she grew to have a repugnance for the wayward habits of her sisters in religion. She developed a love for silence and prayer and this in spite of the fact that the others despised and ridiculed her and called her a fanatic.

It was at this time that a holy priest, who was making the visitation of the convent, had a strange vision while he was making his meditation: he saw a nun in her room, rapt in prayer, kneeling in front of a Lady of breathless beauty who was surrounded by angels. The latter had flaming spears with which they repelled a crowd of devils who wanted to come in. These evil spirits then fled to the other nuns' rooms under the guise of vile animals.

By this vision the priest became aware of the lamentable state the monastery was in and he was so upset that he thought he might almost die of grief. He immediately sent for the young religious and exhorted her to persevere.

As he pondered on the value of the Rosary, he decided to try to reform the sisters by means of it. He bought a supply of beautiful rosaries and gave one to each nun, imploring them to say the Rosary every day, even going so far as to promise them that, if they would only say it faithfully, he would not try to force them to alter their lives. Wonderful and strange as it may seem the nuns agreed to this pact and were glad to be given the rosaries and promised to say them.

Little by little they began to give up their empty and worldly pursuits, letting silence and recollection come into their lives. In less than a year they all asked that the monastery be reformed.

So the Holy Rosary worked more changes in their hearts than the priest could have worked by exhorting and commanding them.

Thirty-Eighth Rose

A Bishop's Devotion

A SPANISH COUNTESS, who had been taught the Holy
Rosary by Saint Dominic, used to say it faithfully
every day with the result that she was making wonderful
strides in her spiritual life. Since her one and only thought
was how she might attain to perfection she asked a Bishop
who was a renowned preacher for some practices that would
help her become perfect.

The Bishop told her that, before he could give her any
counsels, she would have to let him know the state of her
soul and also what her religious exercises were. She
answered that her most important exercise was the Holy
Rosary which she said every day meditating on the Joyous,
Sorrowful and Glorious Mysteries, and that her soul was
greatly helped by so doing.

The Bishop was overjoyed to hear her explain what priceless lessons the mysteries contain. "I have been a doctor of
theology for twenty years," he exclaimed "and I have read
many excellent books on various devotional practices. But
never before have I come across one better than this—for it
is of the essence of Christianity and is a devotion which cannot but bear fruit. I shall follow your example, and from now
on I shall preach the Rosary."

The Bishop's preaching met with great success, for in
almost no time his diocese changed for the better. There was
a notable decline in immorality and worldliness of all kinds
as well as in gambling. There were several striking instances
of people being brought back to the Faith, or sinners making
restitution for their crimes and of others sincerely resolving
to give up lives of vice. Religious fervor and Christian charity began to flourish. These changes were all the more
remarkable because this Bishop had been striving to reform
his diocese for some time but with hardly any results.

To better inculcate devotion of the Rosary, the Bishop

also wore a beautiful rosary at his side and always showed it to the congregation when he preached. He used to say:

"My dear brethren in Jesus Christ, I am a Doctor of Theology and a Doctor of Canon as well as Civil law, but I say to you, as your Bishop, that I take more pride in wearing Our Lady's Rosary than in any of my episcopal regalia or academic robes."

Thirty-Ninth Rose

Parish Transformed

A DANISH PRIEST used to love to tell how the very same improvement that the Spanish Bishop noticed in his diocese had occurred in his own parish. He always told his story with great rejoicing of soul because it gave such glory to Almighty God. He said:

"I had preached as compellingly as I could, touching on many aspects of our Holy Faith, and using every argument I could possibly think of to get the people to amend their way of life. But in spite of all my efforts they went unconcernedly about their way as before; and it was then that I decided to preach the Holy Rosary.

"I told my congregations how precious it is and I taught them how to say it. I kept on preaching the Holy Rosary and the devotion took root in the parish. Six months later I was overjoyed to see that people had really changed for the better. How true it is that this God-given prayer has divine power—the power to touch our hearts and to fill them with horror of sin and the love of virtue!"

One day Our Lady said to Blessed Alan: "Just as Almighty God chose the Angelic Salutation to bring about the Incarnation of His Word and the Redemption of mankind, in the same way those who want to bring about moral reforms and who want people reborn in Jesus Christ must honor me and greet me with the same salutation. I am the channel by which God came to men, and so, next to my Son Jesus Christ, it is through me that men must obtain grace and virtue."

I, who write this, have learned from my own experience that the Rosary has the power to convert even the most hardened hearts. I have known people who have gone to missions and who have heard sermons on the most terrifying subjects without being in the least moved; and yet, after they had, on my advice, started to say the Rosary every day they eventually became converted and gave themselves completely to God.

When I have gone back again to visit parishes where I have given missions I have seen a tremendous difference in them; in those parishes where people had given up the Rosary they had generally fallen back into their sinful ways again, whereas in places where the Rosary was said faithfully I found the people were persevering in the grace of God and were advancing each day in virtue.

Fortieth Rose

Admirable Effects

BLESSED ALAN DE LA ROCHE, Father Jean Dumont, Father Thomas, the chronicles of Saint Dominic and other writers who have seen these things with their own eyes speak of the marvelous conversions that are brought about by the Holy Rosary. Great sinners—both men and women—have been converted after twenty, thirty or even forty years of sin and unspeakable vice, because they persevered in saying the Holy Rosary. And these have been people who, beforehand, had been deaf to all pleading! I shall not tell you about those wonderful conversions here because I do not want to make this book too long. And I am not even going to refer to those which I have seen with my very own eyes: there are several reasons why I would rather not talk about them.[1]

Dear reader, I promise you that if you practice this devotion and help to spread it you will learn more from the Rosary than from any spiritual book. And what is more, you will have the happiness of being rewarded by Our Lady in accordance with the promises that she made to Saint Dominic, to Blessed Alan de la Roche and to all those who practice and encourage this devotion which is so dear to her. For the Holy Rosary teaches people about the virtues of Jesus and Mary, and leads them to mental prayer and to imitate Our Lord and Savior Jesus Christ. It teaches them to approach the Sacraments often, to genuinely strive after Christian virtues and to do all kinds of good works, as well as interesting them in the many wonderful indulgences which can be gained through the Rosary.

People are often quite unaware of how rich the Rosary is in indulgences. This is because many priests, when preaching on the Rosary, hardly ever mention indulgences and give rather a flowery and popular sermon which excites admiration but scarcely teaches anything.

Be that as it may I shall say no more than to assure you, in the words of Blessed Alan de la Roche, that the Holy Rosary is the root and the storehouse of countless blessings. For through the Holy Rosary:

1. Sinners are forgiven;
2. Souls that thirst are refreshed;
3. Those who are fettered have their bonds broken;
4. Those who weep find happiness;
5. Those who are tempted find peace;
6. The poor find help;
7. Religious are reformed;
8. Those who are ignorant are instructed;
9. The living learn to overcome pride;

1. This is an example of Saint Louis' humility! It is more than probable that he himself had extraordinary favors and most likely witnessed miracles—but these he seems reluctant to discuss. M.B.

10. The dead (the Holy Souls) have their pains eased by suffrages.

One day Our Lady said to Blessed Alan:

"I want people who have a devotion to my Rosary to have my Son's grace and blessing during their lifetime and at their death, and after their death I want them to be freed from all slavery so that they will be like kings wearing crowns and with sceptres. in their hands and enjoying eternal glory."

PART II

HOW TO RECITE IT

Forty-First Rose

Purity of Intention

IT IS NOT SO much the length of a prayer, but the fervor with which it is said which pleases Almighty God and touches His Heart. One single Hail Mary that is said properly is worth more than one hundred and fifty that are badly said. Most Catholics say the Rosary, the whole fifteen mysteries or five of them anyway or, at least a few decades. So why is it then that so few of them give up their sins and go forward in the spiritual life? Surely it must be because they are not saying them as they should. It is a good thing to think over how we should pray if we really want to please God and become more holy.

To say the Holy Rosary to advantage one must be in a state of grace or at the very least be fully determined to give up mortal sin. This we know because all our theology teaches us that good works and prayers are only dead works if they are done in a state of mortal sin. Therefore they can neither be pleasing to God nor help us gain eternal life. This is why Ecclesiasticus says: "Praise is not seemly in the mouth of a sinner." (*Ecclus.* 15:9). Praise of God and the salutation of the angel and the very Prayer of Jesus Christ are not pleasing to God when they are said by unrepentant sinners.

Our Lord said: "This people honoreth me with their lips, but their heart is far from me." (*Mark* 7:6). It is as though He was saying: "Those who join My Confraternity and say their Rosary every day (even perhaps the fifteen decades), but without being sorry for their sins offer Me lip service only and their hearts are far from Me."

I have just said that to say the Rosary to advantage one must be in a state of grace "or at least be fully determined to give up mortal sin;" first of all, because, if it were true that God only heard the prayers of those in a state of grace it would follow that people in a state of mortal sin should not pray at all. This is an erroneous teaching which has been condemned by Holy Mother Church, because of course sinners need to pray far more than good people do. Were this horrible doctrine true it would then be useless and futile to tell a sinner to say all, or even part of his Rosary, because it would never help him.

Secondly, because if they join one of Our Lady's confraternities and recite the Rosary or some other prayer, but without having the slightest intention of giving up sin, they join the ranks of her false devotees. These presumptuous and impenitent devotees, hiding under her mantle, wearing the scapular and with rosary in hand, cry out: "Blessed Virgin, good Mother—Hail, Mary! . . ." And yet at the same time, by their sins, they are crucifying Our Lord Jesus Christ and tearing His flesh anew. It is a great tragedy, but from the very ranks of Our Lady's most holy Confraternities souls are falling into the fires of Hell.

We earnestly beg everyone to say the Holy Rosary: the just that they may persevere and grow in God's grace; the sinners that they may rise from their sins. But God forbid that we should ever encourage a sinner to think that Our Lady will protect him with Her mantle if he continues to love sin, for then it will only turn into a mantle of damnation which will hide his sins from the public eye. The Rosary, which is a cure for all our ills, would then be turned into deadly poison. "A corruption of what is best is worst."

The learned Cardinal Hugues says: "One should really be as pure as an angel to approach the Blessed Virgin and to say the Angelic Salutation." One day Our Lady appeared to an immoral man who used to always say his Rosary every day. She showed him a bowl of beautiful fruit, but the bowl itself was covered with filth. The man was horrified to see this, and Our Lady said: "This is the way you are honoring me! You are giving me beautiful roses in a filthy bowl. Do you think I can accept presents of this kind?"

Forty-Second Rose

With Attention

IN ORDER TO pray well, it is not enough to give expression to our petitions by means of that most excellent of all prayers, the Rosary, but we must also pray with real concentration for God listens more to the voice of the heart than that of the mouth. To be guilty of willful distractions during prayer would show a great lack of respect and reverence; it would make our Rosaries fruitless and would make us guilty of sin.

How can we expect God to listen to us if we ourselves do not pay attention to what we are saying? How can we expect Him to be pleased if, while in the presence of His tremendous Majesty, we give in to distractions just as children run after butterflies? People who do this forfeit Almighty God's blessings which are then changed into curses because they have been praying disrespectfully. "Cursed be he that doth the work of the Lord deceitfully." (*Jer.* 28:10).

Of course, you cannot possibly say your Rosary without having a few involuntary distractions and it is hard to say even one Hail Mary without your imagination troubling you a little (for our imagination is, alas, never still). The one thing you can do, however, is to say your Rosary without giving in to distractions deliberately and you can take all sorts of precautions to lessen involuntary distractions and to control your imagination.

With this in mind put yourself in the presence of God and imagine that Almighty God and His Blessed Mother are watching you and that your guardian Angel is standing at your right hand, taking your Hail Marys, if they are well said, and using them like roses to make crowns for Jesus and Mary. But remember that at your left hand lurks the devil ready to pounce upon every Hail Mary that comes his way and to write it down in his deadly notebook. And be sure that he will snatch every single one of your Hail Marys that you have not said attentively, devoutly and with reverence.

Above all, do not forget to offer up each decade in honor of one of the mysteries and while you are saying it try to form a picture in your mind of Jesus and Mary in connection with this mystery.

The life of Blessed Hermann (of the Premonstratensian Fathers) tells us that at one time when he used to say the Rosary attentively and devoutly while meditating upon the mysteries Our Lady used to appear to him resplendent in breathtaking majesty and beauty. But as time went on his fervor cooled and he fell into the way of saying his Rosary hurriedly and without giving it his full attention. Then one day Our Lady appeared to him again—only this time she was far from beautiful and her face was furrowed and drawn with sadness. Blessed Hermann was appalled at the change in her, and then Our Lady explained:

"This is how I look to you, Hermann, because in your soul this is how you are treating me; as a woman to be despised and of no importance. Why do you no longer greet me with respect and attention meditating on my mysteries and praising my privileges?"

Forty-Third Rose

Fighting Distractions

WHEN THE ROSARY is well said it gives Jesus and Mary more glory and it is more meritorious for the soul than any other prayer. But it is also the hardest prayer to say well and to persevere in, owing especially to the distractions which almost inevitably attend the constant repetition of the same words.

When we say the Little Office of Our Lady, or the Seven Penitential Psalms, or any prayers other than the Rosary, the variety of words and expressions keeps us alert, prevents our imagination from wandering, and so makes it easier for us to say them well. On the contrary, because of the constant repetition of the same Our Father and Hail Mary in the same unvarying form, it is difficult, while saying the Rosary, not to become wearied and inclined to sleep or to turn to other prayers that are more refreshing and less tedious. This goes to show that one needs much greater devotion to persevere in saying the Holy Rosary than in saying any other prayer, even the Psalms of David.

Our imagination, which is hardly still a minute, makes our task harder and then of course there is the devil who never tires of trying to distract us and keep us from praying. To what ends does not the evil one go against us while we are engaged in saying our Rosary against him.

Being human, we easily become tired and slipshod—but the devil makes these difficulties worse when we are saying the Rosary. Before we even begin he makes us feel bored, distracted or exhausted—and when we have started praying he oppresses us from all sides. And when, after much difficulty and many distractions, we have finished, he whispers to us: "What you have just said is worthless. It's useless for you to say the Rosary. You had better get on with other things. It's only a waste of time to pray without paying attention to what you're saying; half an hour's meditation or some spiritual reading would be much better. Tomorrow when you're not feeling so sluggish you'll pray better; don't finish your Rosary until tomorrow." By tricks of this kind the devil gets us to give up the Rosary altogether or else hardly say it at all, and we keep putting it off or else change to some other devotion.

Dear Rosary Confraternity members, do not listen to the devil, but be of good heart even if your imagination has been bothering you throughout your Rosary, filling your mind with all kinds of distracting thoughts—as long as you really tried hard to get rid of them as soon as they came. Always remember that the best Rosary is the one with the most merit, and there is more merit in praying when it is hard than when it is easy. Prayer is all the harder when it is (naturally speaking) distasteful to the soul and is filled with those annoying little ants and flies running about in your imagination, against your will, and scarcely allowing you the time to enjoy a little peace and appreciate the beauty of what you are saying.

Even if you have to fight distractions all through your whole Rosary be sure to fight well, arms in hand: that is to say, do not stop saying your Rosary even if it is hard to say and you have absolutely no sensible devotion. It is a terrible battle, I know, but one that is profitable to the faithful soul. If you put down your arms, that is, if you give up the Rosary, you will be admitting defeat and then, having won, the devil will leave you alone.

But at the Day of Judgment he will taunt you because of your faithlessness and lack of courage. "He that is faithful in that which is least, is faithful also in that which is greater." (*Luke* 16:10). He who fights even the smallest distractions faithfully when he says even the very smallest prayer he will also be faithful in great things. We can be absolutely certain of this because the Holy Spirit has told us so.

So all of you, servants and handmaids of Our Lord Jesus Christ and the Blessed Virgin Mary, who have made up your minds to say the Rosary every day, be of good heart. Do not let the flies (it is thus that I call the distractions that make war on you during prayer) make you cowardly abandon the company of Jesus and Mary, in whose holy presence you always are when saying the Rosary. In what follows I shall give you suggestions for getting rid of distractions.

Forty-Fourth Rose

A Good Method

WHEN YOU have asked the Holy Spirit to help you pray well, put yourself for a moment in the presence of God and offer up the decades in the way that I am going to show you later.[1]

Before beginning a decade, pause for a moment or two—depending upon how much time you have—and contemplate the mystery that you are about to honor in that decade. Always be sure to ask of Almighty God, by this mystery and through the intercession of the Blessed Mother, one of the virtues that shines forth most in this mystery or one of which you stand in particular need.

Take great care to avoid the two pitfalls that most people fall into during the Rosary. The first is the danger of not asking for any graces at all, so that if some people were asked their Rosary intention they would not know what to say. So, whenever you say your Rosary, be sure to ask for some special grace. Ask God's help in cultivating one of the great Christian virtues or in overcoming one of your sins.

The second big fault a lot of people make when saying the Holy Rosary is to have no intention other than that of getting it over as quickly as possible! This is because so many of us look upon the Rosary as a burden which is always heavier when we have not said it—especially if it is weighing on our conscience because we have promised to

---

1. See page 195 ff.

say it regularly or have been told to say it as a penance more or less against our will.

It is really pathetic to see how most people say the Holy Rosary—they say it astonishingly fast and mumble so that the words are not properly pronounced at all. We could not possibly expect anyone, even the most unimportant person, to think that a slipshod address of this kind was a compliment and yet we expect Jesus and Mary to be pleased with it! Small wonder then that the most sacred prayers of our holy religion seem to bear no fruit, and that, after saying thousands of Rosaries, we are still no better than we were before! Dear Confraternity members, I beg of you to temper the speed which comes all too easily to you and pause briefly several times as you say the Our Father and Hail Mary. I have placed a cross at each pause, as you will see:

Our Father, Who art in Heaven, † hallowed be Thy name, † Thy kingdom come, † Thy will be done † on earth as it is in Heaven. † Give us this day † our daily bread † and forgive us our trespasses † as we forgive those who trespass against us, † and lead us not into temptation † but deliver us from evil. Amen.

Hail Mary, full of grace, † the Lord is with thee, † blessed art thou among women † and blessed is the Fruit of thy womb, Jesus. †

Holy Mary, Mother of God, † pray for us sinners, now † and at the hour of our death. Amen.

At first, you may find it difficult to make these pauses because of your bad habit of saying prayers in a hurry; but a decade that you say recollectedly in this way will be worth more than thousands of Rosaries said all in a rush—without any pauses or reflection.

Blessed Alan de la Roche and other writers (including Saint Robert Bellarmine) tell the story of how a good confessor advised three of his penitents, who happened to be sisters, to say the Rosary every day without fail for a whole year. This was so that they might make beautiful robes of glory for Our Lady out of their Rosaries. This was a secret that the priest had received from Heaven.

So the three sisters said the Rosary faithfully for a year and on the Feast of the Purification the Blessed Virgin appeared to them at night when they had retired. Saint Catherine and Saint Agnes were with her and she was wearing beautiful robes that shone and all over them "Hail Mary, full of grace" was blazoned in letters of gold. The Blessed Mother came to the eldest sister and said "I salute you, my daughter, because you have saluted me so often and beautifully. I want to thank you for the beautiful robes that you have made me." The two virgin saints who were with Our Lady thanked her too and then all three of them vanished.

An hour later Our Lady and the same two saints appeared to them again, but this time she was wearing green which had no gold lettering and did not gleam. She went up to the second sister and thanked her for the robes she had made Her by saying her Rosary. Since this sister had seen Our Lady appear to the eldest much more magnificently dressed she asked Her the reason for the change. The Blessed Mother answered: "Your sister made Me more beautiful clothes because she has been saying her Rosary better than you."

About an hour after this she appeared to the youngest of the sisters wearing tattered and dirty rags. "My daughter," she said, "I want to thank you for these clothes that you have made Me." The young girl was covered with shame and she called out: "Oh, my Queen, how could I have dressed you so badly! I beg you to forgive me. Please grant me a little more time to make you beautiful robes by saying my Rosary better." Our Lady and the two saints vanished, leaving the girl heartbroken. She told her confessor everything that had happened and he urged her to say her Rosary for another year and to say it more devoutly than ever.

At the end of this second year on the very same day of the Purification, Our Lady, clothed in a magnificent robe and attended by Saint Catherine and Saint Agnes, wearing crowns, appeared to them again in the evening. She said to them: "My daughters, I have come to tell you that you have earned heaven at last—and you will all have the great joy of going there tomorrow." The three of them cried: "Our hearts are all ready, dearest Queen; our hearts are all ready." Then the vision faded. That same night they became ill and so sent for their confessor who brought them the Last Sacraments and they thanked him for the holy practice that he had taught them. After Compline Our Lady appeared with a multitude of virgins and had the three sisters clothed in white gowns. While Angels were singing "Come, spouses of Jesus Christ, receive the crowns which have been prepared for you for all eternity," they departed from this life.

Some very deep truths can be learned from this story:

1. How important it is to have a good director who will counsel holy practices, especially that of the Most Holy Rosary;
2. How important it is to say the Rosary attentively and devoutly;
3. How kind and merciful the Blessed Mother is to those who are sorry for the past and are firmly resolved to do better;
4. And finally, how generous she is in rewarding us in life, death and eternity, for the little services that we render Her faithfully.

Forty-Fifth Rose

With Reverence

I WOULD like to add that the Rosary ought to be said reverently—that is to say it ought to be said, as far as possible, kneeling, with the hands joined and clasping the Rosary. However, if people are ill they can of course say it in bed or if they are travelling it can be said on foot—and if infirmity prevents people kneeling it can be said seated or standing. The Rosary can even be said at work, if people's daily duties keep them at their jobs, because the work of one's hands is not by any means always incompatible with vocal prayer.

Of course, since the soul has its limitations and can only do so much, when we are concentrating on manual work we cannot give our undivided attention to things of the spirit, such as prayer. But when we cannot do otherwise this kind of prayer is not without value in Our Lady's eyes and she rewards our good will more than our external actions.

I advise you to divide up your Rosary into three parts and to say each group of mysteries (five decades) at a different time of day. This is much better than saying the whole fifteen decades all at once.

If you cannot find the time to say a third part of the Rosary all at one time, say it gradually, a decade here and there. I am sure you can manage this; so that, in spite of your work and all the calls upon your time, you will have said the whole Rosary before going to bed.

Saint Francis de Sales sets us a very good example of faith fulness in this respect: once when he was quite exhausted from the visits of the day and remembered, towards midnight, that he had left a few decades of his Rosary unsaid, he would not go to bed until he had finished them on his knees, notwithstanding all the efforts of his secretary who saw he was tired and begged him to let the rest of his prayers go until the next day.

And do let me remind you just once more to copy the faithfulness, reverence and devotion of the holy friar who is mentioned in the Chronicles of Saint Francis and who always said his Rosary very devoutly and reverently before dinner. (I have told this story earlier in this book.)[1]

---

1. Cf. SEVENTH ROSE—Crown of Roses.

Forty-Sixth Rose

Group Recitation

THERE ARE SEVERAL ways of saying the Holy Rosary, but that which gives Almighty God the greatest glory, does the most for our souls and which the devil fears more than any other, is that of saying or chanting the Rosary publicly in two groups.

Almighty God is very pleased to have people gathered together in prayer; the Angels and the blessed unite to praise Him unceasingly. The just on earth in several communities join in communal prayer, night and day. Our Blessed Lord expressly recommended common prayer to His Apostles and disciples and promised that whenever two or three were gathered together in His name He would be there in the midst of them. (Cf. *Matt.* 18:20).

What a wonderful thing to have Jesus Christ in our midst! And the only thing we have to do to get Him to come is to say the Rosary in a group.[2] This is why the early Christians often gathered together to pray in spite of all the Roman Emperor's persecutions and the fact that assemblies were forbidden. They preferred to risk the danger of death rather than to miss their gatherings, at which Our Lord was present.

This way of praying is of the greatest benefit to our souls because:

1. Normally our minds are far more alert during public prayer than they are when we pray alone.
2. When we pray in common, the prayer of each one belongs to us all and these make but one great prayer together, so that if one person is not praying well, someone else in the same gathering who prays better may make up for his deficiency. In this way those who

---

2. St. Louis' message fits in beautifully with that of the great "Family Rosary Crusade" of today. M.B.

are strong uphold the weak, those who are fervent inspire the lukewarm, the rich enrich the poor, the bad are counted as good. How can a measure of cockle be sold? This can be done very easily by mixing it up with four or five barrels of good wheat.

3. Somebody who says his Rosary alone only gains the merit of one Rosary, but if he says it together with thirty other people he gains the merit of thirty Rosaries. This is the law of public prayer. How profitable, how advantageous this is!

4. Urban VIII, who was very pleased to see how devotion to the Holy Rosary had spread in Rome and how it was being said in two groups or choirs, particularly at the convent of Santa Maria Sopra Minerva, attached one hundred days' extra indulgence, toties quoties, whenever the Rosary was said in two choirs. This was set out in his brief *Ad perpetuam rei memoriam,* written in the year 1626. So every time you say the Rosary in two groups you gain one hundred days' extra indulgence.

5. Public prayer is far more powerful than private prayer to appease the anger of God and call down His Mercy and Holy Mother Church, guided by the Holy Ghost, has always advocated public prayer in times of public tragedy and suffering.

In his bull on the Rosary, Pope Gregory XIII says very clearly that we must believe (on pious faith) that the public prayers and processions of members of the Confraternity of the Holy Rosary were largely responsible for the great victory over the Turkish navy at Lepanto which Almighty God granted to Christians on the first Sunday of October, 1571.

When King Louis the Just, of blessed memory, was besieging La Rochelle, where the revolutionary heretics had their stronghold, he wrote to his mother to beg her to have public prayers offered for a victorious outcome. The Queen-Mother decided to have the Rosary recited publicly in Paris in the Dominican Church of Faubourg Saint Honore and this was done by the Archbishop of Paris. It was begun on May 20th, 1628.

Both the Queen-Mother and the reigning Queen attended the recitation of the Rosary together with the Duke of Orleans, Cardinal de La Rochefoucault and Cardinal de Berulle, as well as other prelates. The court turned out in full force as well as a large proportion of the general populace. The Archbishop used to read the meditations on the mysteries aloud and then begin the Our Fathers and Hail Marys of each decade while the congregation made up of religious and lay folk answered him. At the end of the Rosary a statue of the Blessed Mother was solemnly carried in procession while the Litany of Our Lady was sung.

This devotion was kept up with admirable fervor every Saturday and resulted in a manifest blessing from Heaven: for on All Saints' Day of the same year the king defeated the English at the island of Re and made his triumphant entry into La Rochelle. This goes to show the great power of public prayer.

Finally, when people say the Rosary together it is far more formidable to the devil than one said privately, because in this public prayer it is an army that is attacking him. He can often overcome the prayer of an individual, but if this prayer is joined to that of other Christians, the devil has much more trouble in getting the best of it. It is very easy to break a single stick, but if you join it to others to make a bundle it cannot be broken. "In union there is strength." Soldiers join together in an army to overcome their enemies; wicked people often get together for parties of debauchery and dancing, and evil spirits join forces in order to make us lose our souls. So why, then, should not Christians join forces to have Jesus Christ present with them when they pray, to appease Almighty God's anger, to draw down His grace and mercy upon us, and to frustrate and overcome the devil and his angels more forcefully?

Dear Rosary Confraternity members, whether you live in town or in the country, near your parish Church or near a chapel, go there at least every evening (with the parish priest's approval, of course), together with all those who want to recite the Rosary in two choirs. If a Church or a chapel is not available say the Rosary together in your own or a neighbor's house. This is a holy practice which Almighty God, in His mercy, has set up in places where I have preached missions—to safeguard and increase the good brought about by these missions and to prevent further sin.

Before the Holy Rosary took root in these small towns and villages, dances and parties of debauchery went on all the time; dissoluteness, wantonness, blasphemy, quarrels and feuds flourished. One heard nothing but evil songs and doublemeaning talk. But now nothing is heard but hymns and the chant of the Our Father and Hail Mary. The only gatherings to be seen are those of twenty, thirty or a hundred or more people who, at a fixed hour, sing Almighty God's praises just as religious do. There are even places where the Rosary is recited in common—five mysteries at a time—at three special times every day. What a blessing from Heaven this is!

Just as there are wicked people everywhere, do not expect to find that the place you live in is free of them; there will be some who will be certain to avoid coming to Church for the Rosary and they may even make fun of it and will probably do everything in their power to stop you from going, exerting their influence by bad example and bad language. But do not give up. As these wretched souls will have to be separated from God and Heaven for all eternity because their place will be in Hell, already here on earth they have to be separated from the company of Christ Our Lord and His servants and handmaids.

Forty-Seventh Rose

Proper Dispositions

PREDESTINATE SOULS, you who are of God, cut yourselves adrift from those who are damning themselves by their impious lives, laziness and lack of devotion—and, without delay, recite often your Rosary, with faith, with humility, with confidence and with perseverance.

Our Lord Jesus Christ told us to follow His example and to pray always—because of our endless need of prayer, the darkness of our minds, our ignorance and weakness and because of the strength and number of our enemies. Anyone who really gives heed to this Our Master's commandment will surely not be satisfied with saying the Rosary once a year (as the Perpetual Members do) or once a week (like the Ordinary Members) but will say it every day (as a member of the Daily Rosary) and will never fail in this—even though the only obligation he has is that of saving his own soul.

1. "We ought always to pray and not to faint. (*Luke* 18:1). These are the eternal words of our Blessed Lord Himself. And we must believe His words and abide by them if we do not want to be damned. You can understand them in any way you like, as long as you do not interpret them as the world does and only observe them in a worldly way.

Our Lord gave us the true explanation of His words—by means of the example He left us. "I have given you an example that as I have done to you, so you do also." (*John* 13:15). And "He passed the whole night in the prayer of God." (*Luke* 6:12). As though His days were not long enough, He used to spend the night in prayer. Over and over again He said to His Apostles: "Watch ye and pray"; (*Matt.* 26:41); the flesh is weak, temptation is everywhere and always around you. If you do not keep up your prayers, you shall fall . . . And because some of them evidently thought that these words of Our Lord constituted a counsel only they completely missed their point. This is why they fell into temptation and sin, even though they were in the company of Jesus Christ.

Dear Rosary Confraternity members, if you want to lead a fashionable life and belong to the world—by this I mean if you do not mind falling into mortal sin from time to time and then going to Confession, and if you wish to avoid conspicuous sins which the world considers vile and yet at the same time commit "respectable sins"—then, of course, there is no need for you to say so many prayers and Rosaries. You only need to do very little to be "respectable": a tiny prayer at night and morning, an occasional Rosary which may be given to you for your penance, a few decades of Hail Marys said on your Rosary (but haphazardly and without concentration) when it suits your fancy to say them—this is quite enough. If you did less, you might be branded as a freethinker or a profligate; if you did more, you would be eccentric and a fanatic. But if you want to lead a true Christian life and genuinely want to save your soul and walk in the saints' footsteps and never, never, fall into mortal sin—if you wish to break Satan's traps and divert his flaming darts, you must always pray as Our Lord taught and commanded you to do.

If you really have this wish at heart, then you must at least say your Rosary or the equivalent, every day. I have said "at least" because probably all that you will accomplish through your Rosary will be to avoid mortal sin and to overcome temptation. This is because you are exposed to the strong current of the world's wickedness by which many a strong soul is swept away; you are in the midst of the thick, clinging darkness which often blinds even the most enlightened souls; you are surrounded by evil spirits who being more experienced than ever and knowing that their time is short are more cunning and more effective in tempting you.

It will indeed be a marvel of grace wrought by the Most Holy Rosary if you manage to keep out of the clutches of the world, the devil and the flesh and avoid mortal sin and gain Heaven! If you do not want to believe me, at least learn from your own experience. I should like to ask you if, when you were in the habit of saying no more prayers than people usually say in the world and saying them the way they usually say them, you were able to avoid serious faults and sins that were grievous but which seemed nothing much to you in your blindness. Now at last you must wake up, and if you want to live and die without sin, at least mortal sin, pray unceasingly; say your Rosary every day as members always used to do in the early days of the Confraternity.

When our Blessed Lady gave the Holy Rosary to Saint Dominic she ordered him to say it every day and to get others to say it daily. Saint Dominic never let anyone join the Confraternity unless he were fully determined to say it every day. If today people are allowed to be Ordinary Members by saying the Rosary merely once a week, it is because fervor has dwindled, and charity has grown cold. You get what you can out of one who is poor in prayer. "It was not thus in the beginning."

Three things must be stressed here; the first is that if you want to join the Confraternity of the Daily Rosary and share in the prayers and merits of its members, it is not enough to be enrolled in the Ordinary Rosary or just to make a resolution to say it every day; as well as doing this you must give your name to those who have the power to enroll you in it. It is also a very good thing to go to Confession and Holy Communion especially for this intention. The reason for this is that the Ordinary Rosary Membership does not include that of the Daily Rosary, but this latter does include the former.

The second point I want to make is that, absolutely speaking, it is not even a venial sin to fail to say the Rosary every day, or once a week, or even once a year.

The third point is that whenever illness, or work that you have performed out of obedience to a lawful superior or some real necessity, or even involuntary forgetfulness has prevented you from saying your Rosary, you do not forfeit your share in the merits and your participation in the Rosaries of the other Confraternity members. So, absolutely speaking, you are under no obligation to say two Rosaries the next day to make up for the one you missed, as I understand it, through no fault of your own. If, however, when you are ill, your sickness is such that you are still able to say part of your Rosary, you must say that part.

"Blessed are (those) who stand before thee always." (*3 Kgs.* 10:8). "Happy they who dwell in your house! Continually they praise you." (*Ps.* 83:5). "Oh, dear Lord Jesus, blessed are the brothers and sisters of the Daily Rosary Confraternity who are in Thy presence every day—in Thy little home at Nazareth, at the foot of Thy Cross on Calvary, and around Thy throne in Heaven, so that they may meditate and contemplate Thy Joyous, Sorrowful and Glorious Mysteries. How happy they are on earth because of the wonderful graces that Thou dost vouchsafe to them, and how blessed they shall be in Heaven where they will praise Thee in a very special way—for ever and ever!"

2. The Rosary should be said with faith—for our Blessed Lord said: "'Believe that you shall receive; and they shall come unto you." (*Mark* 11:24). If you believe that you will receive what you ask from the hands of Almighty God, He will grant your petitions. He will say to you: "As thou hast believed, so be it done to thee. (*Matt.* 8:13). "If any of, you want wisdom, let him ask of God— but let him ask in faith, nothing wavering." (*James* 1:5, 6). If anyone needs wisdom, let him ask God with faith, and without hesitating, and through his Rosary—and what he asks shall be given him.

3. Thirdly, we must pray with humility, like the Publican; he was kneeling on the ground—on both knees—not on one knee as proud and worldly people do, or with one knee on the bench in front of him. He was at the back of the Church and not in the sanctuary as the Pharisee was; his eyes were cast down, as he dared not look up to Heaven; he did not hold his head up proudly and look about him like the Pharisee. He beat his breast, confessing his sins and asking forgiveness: "Be merciful to me a sinner" (*Luke* 18:13) and he was not in the least like the Pharisee who boasted of his good works and who despised others in his prayers. Do not

imitate the pride of the Pharisee whose prayer only hardened his heart and increased his guilt; imitate rather the humility of the Publican whose prayer obtained for him the remission of his sins.

You should be very careful not to do anything out of the ordinary nor to ask nor even wish for knowledge of extraordinary things, visions, revelations or other miraculous graces which Almighty God has occasionally given to a few of the saints while they were reciting the Rosary. "Faith alone suffices": faith alone is quite enough for us now that the Holy Gospels and all the devotions and pious practices are firmly established.

Even if you suffer from dryness of soul, boredom and interior discouragement, never give up even the least little bit of your Rosary—for this would be a sure sign of pride and faithlessness. On the contrary, like a real champion of Jesus and Mary, you should say your Our Fathers and Hail Marys quite drily if you have to, without seeing, hearing or feeling any consolation whatsoever, and concentrating as best you can on the mysteries. You ought not to look for candy or jam to eat with your daily bread, as children do—but you should even say your Rosary more slowly sometimes when you particularly find it hard to say. Do this to imitate Our Lord more perfectly in His agony in the garden: "Being in an agony, he prayed the longer," (*Luke* 22:43) so that what was said of Our Lord (when He was in His agony of prayer) may be said of you too: He prayed even longer.

4. Pray with great confidence, with confidence based upon the goodness and infinite generosity of God and upon the promises of Jesus Christ. God is a spring of living water which flows unceasingly into the hearts of those who pray. The Eternal Father yearns for nothing so much as to share the life-giving waters of His grace and mercy with us. He is entreating us: "All you that thirst, come to the waters . . ." (*Is.* 54:1). This means "Come and drink of My spring through prayer," and when we do not pray to Him He sorrowfully says that we are forsaking Him: "They have for-

saken me, the fountain of living water." (*Jer.* 2:13). We make Our Lord happy when we ask Him for graces and if we do not ask, He makes a loving complaint: "Hitherto you have not asked anything . . . ask and you shall receive . . . seek and you shall find, knock and it shall be opened to you." (*John* 16:24 and *Matt.* 7:7).

Furthermore, to give us more confidence in praying to Him, He has bound Himself by a promise: that His Eternal Father would grant us everything that we ask in His name.

Forty-Eighth Rose

Perseverance

5. As a fifth point I must add also perseverance in prayer. Only he will receive, will find and will enter who perseveres in asking, seeking and knocking. It is not enough to ask Almighty God for certain graces for a month, a year, ten or even twenty years; we must never tire of asking. We must keep on asking until the very moment of death, and even in this prayer which shows our trust in God, we must join the thought of death to that of perseverance and say: "Although he should kill me, I will trust in him" (*Job* 13:15). and will trust Him to give me all I need.

Prominent and rich people of the world show their generosity by foreseeing people's wants and ministering to them, even before they are asked for anything. On the other hand, God's munificence is shown in His making us seek and ask for, over a long period of time, the grace which He wishes to give us and quite often the more precious the grace, the longer He takes to grant it. There are three reasons why He does this:

1. To thus increase this grace still more:
2. To make the recipient more deeply appreciate it;
3. To make the soul who receives it very careful indeed

not to lose it—for people do not appreciate things that they can get quickly and with very little trouble.

So, dear members of the Rosary Confraternity, persevere in asking Almighty God for all your needs, both spiritual and corporal, through the Most Holy Rosary. Most of all you should ask for divine Wisdom which is an infinite Treasure: "(Wisdom) is an infinite treasure" (*Wis*. 7:14) and there can be no possible doubt that you will receive it sooner or later—as long as you do not stop asking for it and do not lose courage in the middle of your journey. "Thou hast yet a great way to go." (*3 Kgs*. 19:7). This means that you have a long way to go, there will be bad times to weather, many difficulties to overcome and many enemies to conquer before you will have stored up enough treasures of eternity, enough Our Fathers and Hail Marys with which to buy your way to Heaven and earn the beautiful crown which is waiting for each faithful Confraternity member.

"(Let) no man take thy crown": (*Apoc*. 3:11). take care that your crown is not stolen by somebody who has been more faithful than you in saying the Holy Rosary. It is "thy crown"—Almighty God has chosen it for you and you have already won it halfway by means of the Rosaries that you have said well. Unfortunately someone else may get ahead of you in the race—someone who has worked harder and who has been more faithful might possibly win the crown that ought to be yours, paying for it by his Rosaries and good works. All this could really happen if you stand still on the beautiful path where you have been running so well: "You did run well." (*Gal*. 5:7). "Who hath hindered you?" (*Gal*. 5:7). Who is it who will have prevented you from having the Rosary crown? None other than the enemies of the Holy Rosary who are so numerous.

Do believe me, only "the violent bear it away." (*Matt*. 11:12). These crowns are not for timid souls who are afraid of the world's taunts and threats, neither are they for the lazy and indolent who only say their Rosary carelessly, or hastily, just for the sake of getting it over with. The same applies to people who say it intermittently, as the spirit moves them. These crowns are not for cowards who lose heart and down their arms as soon as they see Hell let loose against the Holy Rosary.

Dear Confraternity members: if you want to serve Jesus and Mary by saying the Rosary every day, you must be prepared for temptation: "When thou comest to the service of God . . . prepare thy soul for temptation." (*Ecclus.* 2:1). Heretics and licentious folk, "respectable" people of the world, persons of only surface piety as well as false prophets, hand in glove with your fallen nature and all Hell itself, will wage formidable battles against you in an endeavor to get you to give up this holy practice.

To help you to be better armed against their onslaught, I am going to tell you some of the things these people are always saying and thinking. This is to put you on your guard against them all, but not so much in the case of heretics and out-and-out licentious people, but particularly those who are "respectable" in the eyes of the world, and those who are devout (strange as it may seem) but have no use for the Holy Rosary.

"What is it that this word sower would say?" (*Acts* 17:18). "Come, let us oppress him, for he is against us." That is to say: "What is he doing saying so many Rosaries? What is it he is always mumbling? Such laziness! And what a waste of time to keep sliding those old beads along—he would do much better to work and not be bothered with this foolishness. I know what I'm talking about . . .

"All you have to do, I suppose, is to say your Rosary, and a fortune will fall from Heaven into your lap! The Rosary gives you everything you need without your lifting a finger! But hasn't it been said: 'God helps those who help themselves?' There's no need then of getting mixed up with so many prayers. 'A brief prayer is heard in heaven,' one Our Father and Hail Mary will do provided they are well said.

"God has never told us to say the Rosary—of course it's all

right, it's not a bad devotion when you've got the time. But don't think for one minute that people who say the Rosary are any more sure of Heaven than we are. Just look at the Saints who never said it! Far too many people want to make everybody see through their own eyes: folk who carry everything to extremes, scrupulous people who see sin almost everywhere, making sweeping statements and saying that all those who don't say the Rosary will go to Hell.

"Oh yes, the Rosary is all right for old women who can't read. But surely the Little Office of Our Lady is much more worthwhile than the Rosary? Or the Seven Penitential Psalms? And how could anything be more beautiful than the Psalms which are inspired by the Holy Ghost? You say you have agreed to say the Rosary every day; this is nothing but a fire of straw—you know very well it won't last! Wouldn't it be better to undertake less and to be more faithful about it?

"Come on, my friend, take my word for it, say your morning and night prayers, work hard during the day and offer it up—God doesn't ask any more of you than this. Of course you've got your living to earn; if you were a man of leisure I shouldn't say anything—you could say as many Rosaries as you like then. But as for now, say your Rosary on Sundays and Holy Days when you have lots of time, if you really must say it.

"But really and truly—what are you doing with an enormous pair of beads? You look like an old woman instead of a man! I've seen a little Rosary of only one decade—it's just as good as one of fifteen decades. What on earth are you wearing it on your belt for, fanatic that you are? Why don't you go the whole way and wear it around your neck like the Spaniards? They carry an enormous Rosary in one hand— and a dagger in the other.

"For goodness sake drop those external devotions; real devotion is in the heart . . . etc. etc. . . ."

Similarly, not a few clever people and learned scholars may occasionally try to dissuade you from saying the Rosary (but they are, of course, proud and self willed). They would rather encourage you to say the Seven Penitential Psalms or some other prayers. If a good confessor has given you a Rosary for your penance and has told you to say it every day for a fortnight or a month, all you have to do to get your penance changed to prayers, fasts, Masses or alms, is to go to confession to one of these others.

If you consult certain people in the world who lead lives of prayer, but who have never tried the Rosary, they will not only not encourage it but will turn people away from it to get them to learn contemplation—just as though the Holy Rosary and contemplation were incompatible, just as if all the Saints who have been devoted to the Rosary had not enjoyed the heights of sublime contemplation.

Your nearest enemies will attack you all the more cruelly because you are so close to them. I am speaking of the powers of your soul and your bodily senses—these are distractions of the mind, distress and uncertainty of the will, dryness of the heart, exhaustion and illnesses of the body—all these will combine with the devil to say to you: "Stop saying your Rosary; that is what is giving you such a headache! Give it up; there is no obligation under pain of sin. If you must say it, say only part of it; the difficulties that you are having over it are a sign that Almighty God does not want you to say it. You can finish it tomorrow when you are more in the mood, etc. . . . etc."

Finally, my dear Brother, the Daily Rosary has so many enemies that I look upon the grace of persevering in it until death as one of the greatest favors Almighty God can give us.

Persevere in it and if you are faithful you will eventually have the wonderful crown which is waiting for you in Heaven: "Be thou faithful until death: and I will give thee the crown of life." (*Apoc.* 2:10).

Forty-Ninth Rose

Indulgences

THIS IS THE right time to say a little about indulgences which have been granted to Rosary Confraternity members so that you may gain as many as possible.

Briefly, an indulgence is a remission or relaxation of temporal punishment due to actual sins, by the application of the superabundant satisfactions of Jesus Christ, of the Blessed Virgin Mary and of the saints—which are contained in the Treasury of the Church.

A Plenary Indulgence is a remission of the whole punishment due to sin; a partial indulgence of, for instance, one hundred or one thousand years can be explained as the remission of as much punishment as could have been expiated during one hundred or one thousand years, if one had been given a corresponding number of the penances prescribed by the Church's ancient Canons.

Now these Canons exacted seven and sometimes ten or fifteen years' penance for one single mortal sin, so that a person who was guilty of twenty mortal sins would probably have had to perform a seven year penance at least twenty times, and so on.

Rosary Confraternity members who want to gain the indulgences must:

1. be truly repentant and must go to Confession and Holy Communion, as the Bull of Indulgences teaches;
2. they must be entirely free from affection for venial sin, because if affection for sin is left the guilt is left too, and since the guilt is there, the punishment cannot be lifted;
3. they must say the prayers and carry out the good works designated by the Bull. If, in accordance with what the Popes have said, one can gain a partial indulgence (for instance, of one hundred years) without gaining a Plenary Indulgence, it is not always necessary to go to

Confession and Holy Communion in order to gain it. Such partial indulgences are many of those attached to the Rosary (either of five or of fifteen decades) to processions, blessed Rosaries, etc.

Be sure not to neglect these indulgences. Flammin and a great number of other writers tell the story of a young girl of noble station by the name of Alexandre, who had been miraculously converted and enrolled by Saint Dominic in the Confraternity of the Most Holy Rosary. After her death she appeared to him and said that she had been condemned to seven hundred years of Purgatory, because of her own sins and those that she had made others commit by her worldly ways. So she implored him to ease her pains by his prayers and to ask the Confraternity members to pray for the same end. Saint Dominic did as she had asked.

Two weeks later she appeared to him, more radiant than the sun, having been quickly delivered from Purgatory through the prayers that the Confraternity members had said for her. She also told Saint Dominic that the Holy Souls in Purgatory had given her a message to beg him to go on preaching the Holy Rosary and to beg their relations to offer their Rosaries for them, and that they would reward them abundantly when they came into their glory.

Fiftieth Rose

Various Methods

SO AS TO MAKE the recitation of the Holy Rosary easier for you, here are several methods which will help you to say it in a good and holy way, together with meditation on the Joyful, Sorrowful and Glorious Mysteries of Jesus and Mary. Choose whichever method pleases you and helps you the most: you can make one up yourself, if you like, as several holy people have done before now.

METHODS OF SAYING THE MOST HOLY ROSARY SO AS TO DRAW UPON OUR SOULS THE GRACE OF THE MYSTERIES OF THE LIFE, PASSION AND GLORY OF JESUS, AND MARY

First Method[1]

FIRST, say the "Come, Holy Ghost" and then make your OFFERING OF THE ROSARY:

I unite myself with all the Saints in Heaven, and with all the just on earth; I unite myself with Thee, my Jesus, in order to praise Thy Holy Mother worthily and to praise Thee in her and by her. I renounce all the distractions that may come to me while I am saying this Rosary.

Oh, Blessed Virgin Mary, we offer thee this Creed in order to honor the faith that thou didst have upon earth and to ask thee to have us share in the same faith.

Oh Lord, we offer Thee this Our Father so as to adore Thee in Thy oneness and to recognize Thee as the first cause and the last end of all things.

Most Holy Trinity, we offer Thee these three Hail Marys so as to thank Thee for all the graces which Thou hast given to Mary and those which Thou hast given us through her intercession.

One Our Father, ten Hail Marys, Glory be to the Father . . .

---

1. This method varies slightly from that which is now well known. Saint Louis modified it during his lifetime, but it is given here because it is to be found in the original manuscript of this book.

    The following prayer, revealed to the three children of Fatima by Our Lady of Fatima in 1917, is now added following the Glory be to the Father at the end of each decade:

    O my Jesus, forgive us our sins, save us from the fire of Hell, lead all souls to Heaven, especially those in most need of Thy mercy.

How to Offer Each Decade

The Joyful Mysteries

FIRST DECADE: We offer Thee, O Lord Jesus, this first decade in honor of Thy Incarnation and we ask of Thee, through this mystery and through the intercession of Thy most Holy Mother, a profound humility.

One Our Father, ten Hail Marys, Glory be to the Father . . .

Grace of the mystery of the Incarnation, come down into my soul and make it truly humble.

SECOND DECADE: We offer Thee, O Lord Jesus, this second decade in honor of the Visitation of Thy Holy Mother to her cousin Saint Elizabeth, and we ask of Thee through this mystery and through Mary's intercession, a perfect charity towards our neighbor.

One Our Father, ten Hail Marys, Glory be to the Father . . .

Grace of the mystery of the Visitation come down into my soul and make it really charitable.

THIRD DECADE: We offer Thee, O Child Jesus, this third decade in honor of Thy Blessed Nativity, and we ask of Thee, through this mystery and through the intercession of Thy Blessed Mother, detachment from things of this world, love of poverty and love of the poor.

One Our Father, ten Hail Marys, Glory be to the Father . . .

Grace of the mystery of the Nativity come down into my soul and make me truly poor in spirit.

FOURTH DECADE: We offer Thee, O Lord Jesus, this fourth decade in honor of Thy Presentation in the temple by the hands of Mary, and we ask of Thee, through this mystery and through the intercession of Thy Blessed Mother, the gift of wisdom and purity of heart and body.

One Our Father, ten Hail Marys, Glory be to the Father . . .

Grace of the mystery of the Purification, come down into my soul and make it really wise and really pure.

FIFTH DECADE: We offer Thee, O Lord Jesus, this fifth decade in honor of Thy Finding in the Temple among the learned men by Our Lady, after she had lost Thee, and we ask Thee, through this mystery and through the intercession of Thy Blessed Mother, to convert us and help us amend our lives, and also to convert all sinners, heretics, schismatics and idolaters.

One Our Father, ten Hail Marys, Glory be to the Father . . .

Grace of the mystery of the Finding of the Child Jesus in the Temple, come down into my soul and truly convert me.

The Sorrowful Mysteries

SIXTH DECADE: We offer Thee, O Lord Jesus, this sixth decade in honor of Thy mortal Agony in the Garden of Olives and we ask of Thee, through this mystery and through the intercession of Thy Blessed Mother, perfect sorrow for our sins and the virtue of perfect obedience to Thy Holy Will.

One Our Father, ten Hail Marys, Glory be to the Father . . .

Grace of Our Lord's Agony, come down into my soul and make me truly contrite and perfectly obedient to Thy Will.

SEVENTH DECADE: We offer Thee, O Lord Jesus, this seventh decade in honor of Thy Bloody Scourging and we ask of Thee, through this mystery and through the intercession of Thy Blessed Mother, the grace to mortify our senses perfectly.

One Our Father, ten Hail Marys, Glory be to the Father . . .

Grace of Our Lord's Scourging, come down into my soul and make me truly mortified.

EIGHTH DECADE: We offer Thee, O Lord Jesus, this eighth decade in honor of Thy cruel crowning with thorns, and we ask of Thee, through this mystery and through the intercession of Thy Blessed Mother, a great contempt of the world.

One Our Father, ten Hail Marys, Glory be to the Father . . .

Grace of the mystery of Our Lord's crowning with Thorns, come down into my soul and make me despise the world.

NINTH DECADE: We offer Thee, O Lord Jesus, this ninth decade in honor of Thy carrying Thy Cross and we ask of Thee, through this mystery and through the intercession of Thy Blessed Mother, to give us great patience in carrying our cross in Thy footsteps every day of our life.

One Our Father, ten Hail Marys, Glory be to the Father . . .

Grace of the mystery of the carrying of the Cross, come down into my soul and make me truly patient.

TENTH DECADE: We offer Thee, O Lord Jesus, this tenth decade in honor of Thy Crucifixion on Mount Calvary, and we ask of Thee, through this mystery and through the intercession of Thy Blessed Mother, a great horror of sin, a love of the Cross and the grace of a holy death for us and for those who are now in their last agony.

One Our Father, ten Hail Marys, Glory be to the Father . . .

Grace of the mystery of the Death and Passion of Our Lord and Savior Jesus Christ, come down into my soul and make me truly holy.

The Glorious Mysteries

ELEVENTH DECADE: We offer Thee, O Lord Jesus, this eleventh decade in honor of Thy triumphant Resurrection and we ask of Thee, through this mystery and through the intercession of Thy Blessed Mother, a lively faith.

One Our Father, ten Hail Marys, Glory be to the Father . . .

Grace of the Resurrection come down into my soul and make me really faithful.

TWELFTH DECADE: We offer Thee, O Lord Jesus, this twelfth decade in honor of Thy glorious Ascension, and we ask of Thee, through this mystery and through the interces-

sion of Thy Blessed Mother, a firm hope and a great longing
for Heaven.

One Our Father, ten Hail Marys, Glory be to the Father . . .

Grace of the mystery of the Ascension of Our Lord, come
down into my soul and make me ready for Heaven.

Thirteenth Decade: We offer Thee, O Holy Spirit, this
thirteenth decade in honor of the mystery of Pentecost, and
we ask of Thee, through this mystery and through the intercession of Mary, Thy most faithful Spouse, Thy holy wisdom so that we may know, really love and practice Thy
truth, and make all others share in it.

One Our Father, ten Hail Marys, Glory be to the Father . . .

Grace of Pentecost, come down into my soul and make
me really wise in the eyes of Almighty God.

FOURTEENTH DECADE: We offer Thee, O Lord Jesus, this
fourteenth decade in honor of the Immaculate Conception
and the Assumption of Thy holy and Blessed Mother, body
and soul, into Heaven, and we ask of Thee, through these
two mysteries and through her intercession, the gift of true
devotion to her to help us live and die holily.

One Our Father, ten Hail Marys, Glory be to the Father . . .

Grace of the Immaculate Conception and the Assumption
of Mary, come down into my soul and make me truly
devoted to her.

FIFTEENTH DECADE: We offer Thee, O Lord Jesus, this
fifteenth and last decade in honor of the glorious crowning
of Thy Blessed Mother in Heaven, and we ask of Thee,
through this mystery and through Her intercession, the
grace of perseverance and increase of virtue until the very
moment of death and after that the eternal crown that is prepared for us. We ask the same grace for all the just and for
all our benefactors.

One Our Father, ten Hail Marys, Glory be to the Father . . .

We beseech Thee, dear Lord Jesus, by the fifteen mysteries of Thy life, passion and death, by Thy glory and by the
merits of Thy Blessed Mother, to convert sinners and help
the dying, to deliver the Holy Souls from Purgatory and to

give us all Thy grace so that we may live well and die well—
and please give us the Light of Thy glory later on so that we
may see Thee face to face and love Thee for all eternity.
Amen. So be it.

GOD ALONE

Second Method

A SHORTER WAY

OF COMMEMORATING THE LIFE, DEATH AND
GLORY OF JESUS AND MARY IN THE MOST HOLY
ROSARY, AND A WAY TO CURB OUR
IMAGINATION AND TO LESSEN
DISTRACTIONS

IN ORDER to do this we must add a word or two to each
Hail Mary (depending upon the decade) and this will
help remind us which mystery we are commemorating. This
word or words should be added after the word "Jesus." "And
blessed is the fruit of Thy Womb":

At the 1st Decade	.... "Jesus incarnate"';
At the 2nd "	.... "Jesus sanctifying";
At the 3rd "	.... "Jesus born in poverty";
At the 4th "	.... "Jesus sacrificed";
At the 5th "	.... "Jesus, Saint among saints";
At the 6th "	.... "Jesus in His agony";
At the 7th "	.... "Jesus scourged";
At the 8th "	.... "Jesus crowned with thorns";
At the 9th "	.... "Jesus carrying His Cross";
At the 10th "	.... "Jesus crucified";
At the 11th "	.... "Jesus risen from the dead"

At the 12th	"	. . . . "Jesus ascending to Heaven";
At the 13th	"	. . . . "Jesus filling Thee with the Holy Spirit";
At the 14th	"	. . . . "Jesus raising Thee up";
At the 15th	"	. . . . "Jesus crowning Thee."

At the end of the first five mysteries, we say:

"Grace of the Joyful Mysteries, come down into our souls and make them really holy";

At the end of the second:

"Grace of the Sorrowful Mysteries, come down into our souls and make them truly patient";

And at the end of the third:

"Grace of the Glorious Mysteries, come down into our souls and make them everlastingly happy. Amen."

THE MAIN RULES OF
THE CONFRATERNITY OF
THE MOST HOLY ROSARY

Members should:

1. Have their names written in the Confraternity book, and, if possible, go to Confession and Holy Communion and say the Holy Rosary the same day that they are enrolled;

2. Have a blessed rosary;

3. Say the Holy Rosary every day or at least once a week;

4. Whenever possible, go to Confession and Holy Communion the First Sunday of every month, and assist at the Holy Rosary Processions.

Remember that none of these rules binds under pain of even venial sin.

The Power, Value and Holiness of the Rosary

A Revelation of our Blessed Lady to Blessed Alan de la Roche

THROUGH THE ROSARY, hardened sinners of both sexes became converted and started to lead a holy life, bemoaning their past sins with genuine tears of contrition. Even children performed unbelievable penances; devotion to my Son and to me spread so thoroughly that it almost seemed as though angels were living on earth. The Faith was gaining, and many Catholics longed to shed their blood for it and fight against the heretics. Thus, through the sermons of my very dear Dominic and through the power of the Rosary, the heretics' lands were all brought under the Church. People used to give munificent alms; hospitals and churches were built. People led moral and law-abiding lives and worked wonders for the glory of God. Holiness and unworldliness flourished; the clergy were exemplary, princes were just, people lived at peace with each other and justice and equity reigned in the guilds and in the homes.

Here is an even more impressive thing: workmen did not take up their tools until they had said my Psalter and they never went to sleep at night without having prayed to me on their knees. If they happened to remember that they had not paid me this tribute they would get up—even in the middle of the night—and then would salute me with great respect and remorse.

The Rosary became so widespread and so well-known that people who were devoted to it were always considered by others as obviously being Confraternity members. If a man lived openly in sin, or blasphemed, it was quite the usual thing to say:

"This man cannot possibly be a brother of Saint Dominic."

I must not fail to mention the signs and wonders that I have wrought in different lands through the Holy Rosary: I have stopped pestilences and put an end to horrible wars as well as to bloody crimes, and through my Rosary people have found the courage to flee temptation.

When you say your Rosary the angels rejoice, the Blessed Trinity delights in it, my Son finds joy in it too, and I myself am happier than you can possibly guess. After the Holy Sacrifice of the Mass, there is nothing in the Church that I love as much as the Rosary.

(Blessed Alan)

Having been strongly urged to do so by Saint Dominic, all the brothers and sisters of his order honored my Son and me unceasingly and in an indescribably beautiful way by saying the Holy Rosary.

Every day each one of them said at least one complete Rosary. If anybody failed to say it he felt that his day was entirely spoiled.

The Brothers of Saint Dominic had so great a love for this holy devotion that it made them do everything better and they used to hurry to church or to the choir to sing the office. If one of them was seen to carry out his duties carelessly the others would say with assurance:

"Oh, Brother! Either you are not saying Mary's Psalter any more or else you are saying it badly."

The Salutation of the Rosary Is Worthy of the Queen of Heaven

"THE HOLY ANGELS in Heaven salute the most Blessed Virgin with the Hail Mary—not audibly, but with their angelic intelligences. For they are fully aware that through it reparation was made for the fallen Angels' sin, God was made man and the world was renewed." (Blessed Alan).

One night when a woman Confraternity member had retired, Our Lady appeared to her and said:

"My daughter, do not be afraid of me. I am your loving Mother whom you praise so faithfully every day. Be steadfast and persevere; I want you to know that the Angelic Salutation gives me so much joy that no man could ever really explain it."

(Guillaume Pepin, in Rosario aureo Sermon 47)

Saint Gertrude corroborated this in one of her visions; in her Revelations, Book IV, Chapter II, we find this story:

It was the morning of the feast of the Annunciation and the Hail Mary was of course being sung in Saint Gertrude's monastery. During the singing she had a vision in which three streams gushed forth from the Father, the Son and the Holy Ghost and gently flowed into Mary's virginal heart. The minute they reached her heart they bounded back to the source from where they had come.

From this Saint Gertrude learned that the Blessed Trinity has allowed Our Lady to be most powerful next to God the Father, the wisest after God the Son, and the most loving after God the Holy Ghost. She also learned that every time the

Angelic Salutation is said by the faithful the three mysterious streams surround Our Lady in a mighty, swirling current and rush into her heart. After they have completely bathed her in happiness they gush back into the bosom of Almighty God. The Saints and Angels share in this abundance of joy as do the faithful on earth, who say this prayer. For the Angelic Salutation is the source of all good for God's children.

This is what Our Lady herself said to Saint Gertrude:

"Never has any man composed anything more beautiful than the Hail Mary. No salutation could be dearer to my heart than those beautiful and dignified words that God the Father addressed to me Himself."

One day Our Lady said to Saint Mechtilde:

"All the Angelic Salutations that you have given me are blazoned on my cloak." (Then she held out a portion of her mantle.) "When this part of my cloak is full of Hail Marys I shall gather you up and take you into the Kingdom of my Beloved Son."

Denis the Carthusian, speaking of a vision of Our Lady to one of her clients, said:

"We should salute the most Blessed Virgin with our hearts, our lips, and our deeds, so that she will not be able to say to us:

" 'These people honor me with their lips, but their hearts are far from me.' "

Richard of Saint Laurent lists the reasons why it is good to say a Hail Mary at the beginning of a sermon:

1. The Church Militant should follow the example of Saint Gabriel who saluted Mary with great respect saying the Hail Mary, before he told her the joyous tidings: "Behold thou shalt conceive and bear a son . . ." Thus the Church salutes the Blessed Virgin before announcing the Gospel.

2. The congregation will derive more fruit from a sermon that is prefaced by the Hail Mary; the priest who gives the sermon has the Angel's role as it were. But in order that the congregation may give birth to Christ in their souls (by faith)

they must first of all obtain this grace from the Blessed Virgin who gave birth to Him the first time, and together with her they will become the Mothers of the Son of God. For without Mary they cannot produce Jesus in their souls.

3. The Gospels show up the power of the Hail Mary; people will get help from Our Lady through this prayer.

4. To say it is a great safeguard and a way of avoiding dangerous pitfalls: Mary, our Illuminatrix, gives light to preachers.

5. The members of the congregation, following Our Lady's example, listen more attentively and are more apt to remember God's words.

6. The devil (who is the enemy of the human race and of the preaching of the Gospel) is driven off by the Hail Mary. This is most necessary because, to quote Our Lord's words, there is danger of his coming to take the word of God out of people's hearts, "lest believing they might be saved."

In his first sermon on the Holy Rosary Clement Losoun says:

"After Saint Dominic had gone to Heaven devotion to the Rosary waned until it was very nearly dead, when a terrible pestilence broke out in several parts of the country. The wretched people sought the advice of a saintly hermit who lived in the desert in great austerity. They besought him to intercede to Almighty God for them. So the hermit called upon the Mother of God, imploring her, as Advocate of Sinners, to come to their aid.

"Our Lady then appeared and said: 'These people have stopped singing my praises. This is why they have been visited with such a scourge. If they will only go back to the ancient devotion of the Most Holy Rosary, they will enjoy my protection. I shall see to their salvation if only they win sing the Rosary, for I love this type of chanting.'

"So the people did what Mary asked and made themselves rosaries, which they started saying with all their heart and soul."

Indulgences

An indulgence is the remission before God of the temporal punishment due for sins which have already been forgiven as far as their guilt is concerned. Indulgences are granted by God through the Catholic Church which, as minister of the Redemption, dispenses and applies the treasury of the satisfaction won by Christ and the Saints.

Though the guilt of sin and the eternal punishment it may have merited are remitted by sacramental absolution, measurable punishment before or after death is still required in order to satisfy God's justice, even for sins already forgiven. To the extent we fail to atone sufficiently for our sins during our lifetimes on earth, we will suffer for a given "time" in Purgatory. An indulgence cancels or lessens this non-eternal punishment.

In order to gain an indulgence, one must be baptized, not excommunicated, and in the state of grace at least at the completion of the prescribed work. In order to gain indulgences, one must have at least a general intention of gaining them. If at the beginning of the day we make an intention to gain all the indulgences we can that day, we do not have to make this intention each time we perform a work to which an indulgence is attached. An indulgence may be gained for oneself or may be offered for souls in Purgatory, but may not be applied to another living person.

A *plenary indulgence* remits all the punishment due for sin and makes possible immediate entrance into Heaven after death.

The New Norms

To gain a plenary indulgence, it is necessary to perform the work to which the indulgence is attached and to fulfill three conditions: sacramental Confession, Eucharistic Communion, and prayer for the intentions of the Pope. (The recitation of one Our Father and one Hail Mary fully suffices, though we are free to recite any other prayer we desire.) It is further required that all attachment to sin, even venial sin, be absent. If this disposition is in any way less than complete, or if the three prescribed conditions are not fulfilled, the indulgence will be only partial.

The three conditions may be fulfilled several days before or several days after performing the prescribed work; nevertheless, it is fitting that Communion be received and prayer for the Pope's intentions be said the same day the work is performed.

A single Confession suffices for gaining several plenary indulgences. However, one must receive Holy Communion and pray for the Pope's intentions for each plenary indulgence. To be able to gain a daily plenary indulgence, one should go to Confession at least every two weeks.

Only one plenary indulgence can be acquired each day, unless a person is at the point of death. In that event, even after gaining a plenary indulgence that day, one can gain the plenary indulgence *for the moment of death.*

A *partial indulgence* remits only part of the punishment due for sin and is now granted without designation of a specific number of "days" or "years." The faithful who, at least with a contrite heart, perform an action or recite a prayer to which a partial indulgence is attached, obtain, in addition to the remission of temporal punishment acquired by the action itself, an equal remission of punishment through the intervention of the Church. The amount remitted depends on the person's fervor, on the greatness of the sacrifice, and on how perfectly the act is performed. Any number of partial indulgences can be acquired per day, unless otherwise indicated.

Indulgences for Praying the Rosary

A plenary indulgence is granted for reciting five decades of the Rosary in a Catholic church or in a family group, religious community or pious association. (A partial indulgence is granted in other circumstances.) The five decades must be recited continuously. The vocal recitation must be accompanied by pious meditation on the mysteries. In public recitation, the mysteries must be announced in the manner customary in the place; for private recitation, however, it suffices if the vocal recitation is accompanied by meditation on the mysteries.

Confraternity of the Most Holy Rosary

To enroll in the Confraternity and receive its many benefits under the special protection of Our Lady, write to one of the following: National Director, Rosary Confraternity, 141 East 65th Street, New York, N.Y. 10021, *or* Confraternity of the Most Holy Rosary, Rosary Center, P.O. Box 3617, Portland, OR 97208.

WHY THE ROSARY?

A FEW GOOD REASONS

For world peace
"Say the Rosary every day, to obtain peace for the world."
—*Our Lady of Fatima,* 1917.

In his encyclical *Mense Maio* ("In the Month of May"), Pope Paul VI urged Christians to pray to Our Lady Queen of Peace for world peace. He laid special emphasis on the Rosary, "the prayer so dear to Our Lady and so highly recommended by the Supreme Pontiffs."

A means for preserving the home
"There is no surer means of calling down God's blessings upon the family . . . than the daily recitation of the Rosary."   —*Pope Pius XII.*

"If families will but listen to my message and give Our Lady ten minutes of their twenty-four hours by reciting the daily Family Rosary, I assure them that their homes will become, by God's grace, peaceful, prayerful places—little heavens, which God the Author of home life has intended they should be!"
                                        —*Father Peyton.*

For courage in the hardships of life
". . . a powerful means of renewing our courage will undoubtedly be found in the Holy Rosary . . ."
                                        —*Pope Leo XIII.*

As a ready and easy means of preserving the Faith
". . . We have elsewhere brought it to the attention of the devout Christian that not least among the advantages of the Rosary is the ready means it puts in his hands to nurture his faith. and to keep him from ignorance of his religion and the danger of error."   —*Pope Leo XIII.*

WHY THE ROSARY?

For healing the evils of our day
"We do not hesitate to affirm again publicly that We put great confidence in the Holy Rosary for the healing of evils which afflict our times."   —*Pope Pius XII*

A means of Christian perfection
". . . Therefore we are sure that Our children and all their brethren throughout the world will turn (the Rosary) into a school for learning true perfection, as, with a deep spirit

of recollection, they contemplate the teachings that shine forth from the life of Christ and of Mary Most Holy."

—Pope John XXIII

For success in one's vocation in life

"I think that I did not miss a single day in reciting it, including the most terrible times of battle when I had no rest night or day. How often did I see her manifest intercession in the decisions which I made in choosing a precise tactic. Take, then, the advice of an old soldier seasoned by experience: Do not neglect the recitation of the Rosary for any reason."

—Marshal Foch, great military leader of WWI

As a powerful means of obtaining graces from God

"Among all the devotions approved by the Church none has been favored by so many miracles as the devotion of the Most Holy Rosary." *—Pope Pius IX*

For final perseverance

"Those who say it fervently and frequently will gradually grow in grace and holiness and will enjoy the special protection of Our Lady and the abiding friendship of God.

"No one can live continually in sin and continue to say the Rosary—either he will give up sin or he will give up the Rosary." *—Bishop Hugh Boyle*

ACT OF CONSECRATION TO THE IMMACULATE HEART OF MARY
(St. Louis De Montfort's Consecration)

"I. N., a faithless sinner—renew and ratify today in thy hands, O Immaculate Mother, the vows of my Baptism; I renounce forever Satan, his pomps and works; and I give myself entirely to Jesus Christ, the Incarnate Wisdom, to carry my cross after Him all the days of my life, and to be more faithful to Him than I have ever been before.

"In the presence of all the heavenly court I choose thee this day, for my Mother and Mistress. I deliver and consecrate to thee, as thy slave, my body and soul, my goods, both interior and exterior, and even the value of all my good actions, past, present and future; leaving to thee the entire and full right of disposing of me, and all that belongs to me, without exception, according to thy good pleasure, for the greater glory of God, in time and in eternity. Amen."

Nihil Obstat: Thomas W. Smiddy, S.T.D., Cen. Lib.
Imprimatur: ✠ Thomas Edmunds Molloy, Bishop of Brooklyn

PRAYER TO ST. MICHAEL
(Promulgated by Pope Leo XIII)

St. Michael, the archangel, defend us in battle; be our protection against the malice and snares of the devil. We humbly beseech God to command him, and do thou, O prince of the heavenly host, by the divine power thrust into hell Satan and the other evil spirits who roam through the world seeking the ruin of souls. Amen.

PRAYER FOR THE POPE

May the Lord preserve our *Holy Father Pope Benedict XVI*, give him life, and make him blessed upon earth, and deliver him not to the will of his enemies.

LET US PRAY: O God, the Shepherd and Ruler of all the faithful, in Thy mercy look down upon Thy servant, Benedict, whom Thou hast appointed to preside over Thy Church, and grant we beseech Thee that both by word and example he may edify those who are under his charge; so that, with the flock entrusted to him, he may attain life everlasting. Through Christ our Lord. Amen.

Kindly include in your daily prayers our president and government officials.

Dear Reader,

Having finished reading *The Secret of the Rosary*, you are called upon by Our Lady to *act* and to apply these soul-stirring instructions in your daily life. The world is still in grave peril from the well-organized anti-Christian forces that have captured, it would seem, all of society throughout the world in a hideous net of subsistence-level poverty, welfare statism, licentiousness and ignorance of Christ's truth. And the Church is equally in peril from the enemy within, who seeks to disarm her by refusing to return to our ancient, life-giving traditions and by suggesting that we should abandon the Holy Rosary. Pope Paul VI hinted at this infiltration when he said it seemed that "The smoke of Satan has entered the temple of God."

The Communists have "played possum," pretending to disband and allow freedom. Yes, they have allowed some personal and economic freedoms, but the same behind-the-scenes forces still control things, and the governments of the West, especially of the U.S.A., are disarming unilaterally in the face of a wily enemy.

Were any of the Free World's great powers in the 20th century able to stem the advance of Communism—the direst foe of God in all history? But where man has failed, history records that the Rosary alone has succeeded. Austria, Brazil, Chile and Portugal all saved themselves from the peril of Communism by the recitation of the Rosary. (Read *Fatima—The Great Sign* for proof.) St. Louis De Montfort tells us (p. 97) that the Rosary was largely responsible for the crucial victory over the Turks at Lepanto in October, 1571.

Another signal victory like that at Lepanto can be won today, *if enough people will respond here and now* to Our Lady's requests to do penance in reparation for sin (the cause of all wars) and especially to "pray the Rosary every day." Our Lady told the children of Fatima to "pray the Rosary every day in honor of Our Lady of the Rosary, in order to obtain peace for the world and the end of the war, because only she can help you." For all the vast paraphernalia of power politics are but a shadow compared with the infinite power of the Rosary before God, *provided it is fervently used and propagated.*